KARA GRAND

HOW TO BECOME A FLIGHT ATTENDANT

for airlines in the Middle East

Copyright and Internet Resources Notice

This book is copyrighted with all rights reserved. It is illegal to copy, distribute or create derivative works from this book in whole or in part, or to contribute to the copying, distribution or creating of derivatives from this book. No part of this book may be reproduced, stored in a retrieval system or transmitted in any form or by any means, electronic, mechanical, photocopying, recording or otherwise, without express written permission of the author.

When you purchased the book, you agreed that the information contained in this book is an expression of opinion. You are responsible for your own behavior, and none of this book is considered legal, medical or personal advice.

CONTENTS

Welcome to the amazing world of flying! 1
Chapter 1 - What are you getting into 4
   1.1 The life of a flight attendant 4
   1.2 Your prospect employer 8
   1.3 Who is hiring 9
   1.4 Your worries and questions answered 9
Chapter 2 - Let's get you the job 17
   2.1 Before the assessment 18
   2.1.1 Creating your CV 18
   2.1.2 Application photos 29
   2.1.3 Online application 33
   2.1.4 Online video interview 33
   2.2 The assessment 35
   2.2.1 How to dress for your assessment day 35
   2.2.2 How to be confident during the assessment day 38
   2.2.3 Documents 42
   2.2.4 Open Day 42
   2.2.5 CV Submission Day 44
   2.2.6 Assessment Day 45
   2.2.6.1 Introduction 47
   2.2.6.2 Reach test 47
   2.2.6.3 The group exercise 48
   2.2.6.3.1 Exercise 1 - Customer Service Scenarios and Role Play 49
   2.2.6.3.2 Exercise 2 - One Word Cards 55
   2.2.6.3.3 Exercise 3 - Prioritization 58
   2.2.6.3.4 Exercise 4 - Team Building 62
   2.2.6.4 English Test 65
   2.2.6.4.1 Grammar Tests 65

250 Missing Words Sample Practice Test 66
Fill-in the blanks Sample Practice Test 1 109
Fill-in the blanks Sample Practice Test 2 110
Fill-in the blanks Sample Practice Test 3 111
Fill-in the blanks Sample Practice Test 4 112
30-Sentence "fill-in-the-blanks" Sample Practice Test 113
40-Sentence Rephrase Sample Practice Test 115
2.2.6.4.2 Reading and understanding test 120
Sample Practice Test 1 120
2Sample Practice Test 2 121
Sample Practice Test 3 123
Sample Practice Test 4 125
Sample Practice Test 5 126
2.2.6.4.3 Essay writing 129
SAMPLE PRACTICE ESSAY 129
SAMPLE PRACTICE ESSAY TOPICS 130
2.2.6.5 Math Test 131
SAMPLE PRACTICE MATH TEST 131
2.2.6.6 Psychometric Test 137
2.2.6.7 Raven test (IQ test) 137
2.2.7. Final Interview 138
2.2.7.1 Making a good impression during the interview 139
2.2.7.2 101 Question and Answers for the Final Interview 140
2.3 After the assessment 242
2.3.1 Golden Call and Successful Candidate Email 242
2.3.2 Document submission 243
2.3.3 Date of Joining (DOJ) 244
2.3.4 Documents to prepare for your departure 244

Chapter 3 – Off you go! 245

3.1 Family and friends 245
3.2 What to pack 246
3.3 New place called home 247
3.4 The training 247

See you up there! 250

WELCOME TO THE AMAZING WORLD OF FLYING!

The perfect candidate is an adventurous, passionate person, easily bored in a monotonous environment, willing to relocate to the Middle East and start working in the airline industry as a flight attendant (by far the most amazing job in the world!).

In this book, we will be discussing the expat cabin crew lifestyle, as these airlines present the most advantages for the employees, ranging from working hours and schedule to paid uniform, accommodation and transport, bonuses and a cosmopolitan lifestyle. While the advice in this book can be used to succeed in any flight attendant interview, every airline has different general requirements for recruiting cabin crew.

In here, you will learn about the interview process for Emirates, Etihad Airways, and Qatar Airways. I am not advertising any of the companies, and no one can say that one is better than the other. It is your decision to make who you wish to work for. All three airlines are excellent with their employees and customers, and you will gain amazing experience working for either one of them.

I have been working in the aviation industry for seven years, as a cabin crew and purser. From the first month of flying, until the last moment, I could not believe that at the end of each amazing month of travel I will still get paid more than I could have made anywhere else.

I have seen 52 countries without counting the ones where we just arrived at the airport and departed 1 hour later. I met the man who would become my husband on one of my flights.

I served and talked to princesses, sheiks, rock stars, F1 drivers, best-selling authors, a holder of Nobel Peace Prize and a blond socialite whose name I cannot divulge. It has been the most exciting period of my life. I embarked on a new and very different adventure when I decided to stop flying to raise my three children.

But before all of this, I was just like you: dreaming of maybe one day being a cabin crew, travel and experience the world with all that it has to offer. I struggled to understand how the interviews work and what makes some people successful and some unsuccessful. I was frustrated and could not understand what they were looking for. One day, however, I realized what the secret was, and that's when I finally got the job.

I know that so many of you are a perfect fit for this career and lifestyle. I wanted to help as many people as I could, so I created the website www.FlightAttendantCentral.com. It started in 2011 as a small blog with a couple of articles, and it turned into an amazing community of talented people who were all aiming high and following their dream to work in the sky.

This is how this book came to life. Based on real answers, practical scenarios, exercises and what you need to succeed, I covered every single possible aspect so you can be successful at the interview from your first try.

The first edition was released in 2012, the second was published in 2013, and the next was released in January 2016.

This revision includes updated information about each airline, the online application process, a new chapter explaining the online video interview, new Group Exercises, new English Tests, a Math Test and an updated list of questions and answers.

I've put my heart and soul into this book, and I hope you enjoy it.

I love hearing from my readers, whether it is to hear your success stories or answer your questions.

You can always contact me at kara@flightattendantcentral.com

How to use this book

This book is designed as a handbook. You will probably not read it all at one time, but rather go to the chapters that are of interest to you at a certain time. Read the Assessment Day chapter before your big day or go through the 101 Questions and Answers before your Final Interview.

Chapter 1 describes the life of a flight attendant. At the end of the chapter is the very popular topic "Your worries and questions answered" that clarifies aspects such as tattoos, minimum and maximum age, marital status or swimming skills.

Chapter 2 will get you deep into the interview process. You will learn how to create your CV, how your application photos should look like, what is a CV drop-off Day, Open Day or an Invitation Only Assessment Day, (and how should you prepare for them), what you should know about the group exercise (including examples of exercises and how you should approach them), English tests, math test, IQ test, personality profile test and the final interview. Here you will also learn how to be confident during the interview and how long you have to wait to get an answer. The chapter ends with the paperwork you need to prepare to join the airline.

In Chapter 3 we will discuss what comes after the interview, how to handle the relocation, what to pack and what to expect once you get there. Also, you will know what kind of information you will learn during the training.

Print out chapters like "101 Questions and Answers for the Final Interview" and all the "English Tests", "Math Test" or "Group Exercises." It will help you see the exercises better and write down your own answers. Or you can print it all and take it with you when you go for the interview.

CHAPTER 1 - WHAT ARE YOU GETTING INTO

1.1 THE LIFE OF A FLIGHT ATTENDANT

I will present to you a list of the greatest aspects of being a flight attendant, as well as the less glamorous parts of the job. You must make an informed decision when choosing this career.

Pros

Being a flight attendant has enormous benefits, especially when you are young and adventurous.

1. See the world at no cost to you

The airlines in the Middle East have impressive route maps. Whatever destination farther than 5 hours flight away implies that the crew will have a layover in that city. Depending on the flight frequency, your length of stay could be anything from 18 to 100 hours. All expenses paid and you can discover the city, do some sightseeing, see concerts, explore restaurants, and whatever else brings you joy.

2. Meet awesome people

Many airlines pride themselves on the number of nationalities they employ. My airline had more than 120 nationalities. You will meet people from countries you never knew existed (Faroe Islands anyone?) to countries that seem far and exotic, such as Japan, Nicaragua, Luxembourg, Paraguay, Azerbaijan or Eritrea.
Not only your colleagues, but also your passengers are from all over the world, and everybody has a unique story to tell. All you have to do is listen and open your heart!

3. Broaden your mind and experiences

One of my colleagues had a small book in which she was writing the same five phrases in all the languages that people she met were speaking. What a collection she built!

I met a girl from Finland who started studying Arabic, and in 1 year she was able to have conversations with native speakers.

Another amazing woman was going to Nepal every time she had some days off. She was collecting and bringing supplies to local schools and spending some time with children who are so poor they have never even seen a TV set.

My friend Nadine went to Traditional Massage School in Thailand and got herself a diploma on how to be a real Thai massage therapist.

You go, you see, your mind and heart grow. This job gives you continuous opportunities to find passions and hobbies that you will never be able to pursue at home with a 9-5 job and two weeks of vacation per year.

4. Free time

Every month you will get 8 to 12 days off. Having all the time, resources and quietness, you will manage to do many things while you are flying: dreams, education or passions.

5. Flexible ever-changing team and environment

If you work with Maxine who is not the nicest person or the most helpful colleague, that is ok. You will not see her the next day at work, or next week or even next month! Hey, if all stars align, you might never have to see Maxine again.

Also, no two flights are the same. If today you serve croissants and coffee, tomorrow you will serve steak. Today your flight is 2 hours; tomorrow it might be 8 hours. Monday you sleep at home, and Tuesday in a hotel in Brussels. No two days are alike. If you don't like monotony, this will be a fantastic experience.

This was one of the biggest revelations for me. I loved it!

6. Your accommodation, transportation, and uniform will be taken care of

The airlines in the Middle East offer their cabin crew housing in the newest and most modern buildings in the city. You will have to share a two or three bedroom apartment with a flatmate. The airline will keep in mind either your request to move in with a training colleague (batch mate) or based on your preferences (smoking/nonsmoking, vegetarian/non-vegetarian, same nationality, etc.). This is great, particularly in the beginning when you do not know many people, there will be somebody to come home to, talk and eat together.

Transportation to and from the airport is provided in the company buses. You will be picked up from your accommodation building and dropped off at the airport. The door to door service.

A full set of uniform - jackets, a week supply of blouses, skirts, pants, scarves, ties, cardigans, suitcases, handbags, as well as shoes and sometimes even pantyhose is given to the cabin crew at the beginning of service. There will be yearly replacements of items such as shoes and clothing.

7. People will be admiringly staring at you and your colleagues when walking through airports

The uniform and the airport is for a flight attendant what a bikini and the runway is for a swimsuit model. People will go out of your way, take pictures of you, hold their children up so they can see the "pretty ladies", whistle and wave. It is an amazing feeling. You will feel proud, important and admired.

8. Staff travel

Every airline offers its employees the opportunity to buy tickets at 90% discount (plus airport taxes). They are called ID90, and while you will only be accepted for travel if there are available seats (and most of the time there will be a vacant seat), it is the cheapest way to see the world. You can use them to fly with your airline or with partner airlines. And because you might have 4 or 5 days off in a row, why not visit the pyramids in Cairo, the ancient city of Petra or beautiful Athens in these days?

9. Discounts everywhere

Every year my airline provided us with a thick book of coupons. They were discount cards for various shops and services. They range from sunglasses to make-up, restaurants and even laser treatments or teeth whitening. I even got 10% off the price of my car when I flashed my crew badge.

Cons

There is always the reverse of the coin. This is an honest analysis of the hard times and what you should expect in between the glamor and jet-setting.

1. Away from home and family

While we all strive for independence and finally leave the bedroom that still has traces of your childhood, there will be times when what you miss most will be your mother's cooking or the non-ending chats with your friends. Most of the times you will make friends with your colleagues who are in the same training program. You will most likely find people from your country and be able to speak your native language and bond. But you will miss your home for a while. It happens until the first time you go back, a time when you start referring to your new base as "home."

Also, by keeping in touch with your family and friends via emails, Skype or Facebook, you will still find meaningful time together.

2. Flexible ever-changing team and environment

While this is also an advantage, it has its disadvantages. When you meet and work with people that you like and get along with very well, you will want to continue seeing them at work every time you go. That is of course not possible.

See the people you like outside work. Maybe you will not get a permanent colleague but gain a friend.

3. Health

Flying puts quite a lot of stress on your body. You will need to pay extra attention to how you take care of yourself, from your skin, hydration, weight management, blood circulation and flu&cold prevention. You will quickly learn the secrets of staying in top notch shape and be in your best physical condition.

4. Relationships

Some of your friends might understand that you cannot attend their weekend party or birthday gathering because you have a night flight. Your partner might be open to the fact that you are gone ten days at a time. At a certain point, however, this will start weighing on you. You will want to be present, not miss out important events and spend more time with friends. This is perfectly normal, and you should always do your best to make up for what you were missing by buying a coffee or drink for your friend whose birthday you missed and spend the most time you can with your loved one.

5. Holidays

This is a difficult one. Flights do not get canceled on Christmas Eve, New Year's Day, Chinese New Year, Eid or Diwali. As unimaginable as it sounds right now, you will sometimes have to go to work on December 31 at 10 PM to operate that flight to Hong Kong. Your friends will be ready for the party, your boyfriend or girlfriend will be sad because the only thing to kiss at midnight will be just a picture of you, but there is nothing you can do about it. In the aircraft you will wish people Happy New Year, at midnight local time over whichever country you fly over, the pilots will make a public announcement wishing everybody a Happy New Year and you will cheer in the galley with your colleagues over a glass of Ginger Ale, not because you particularly like the taste, but because it has the same color as champagne.

From all the pitfalls of this amazing job, personally, this was by far the most difficult to deal with.

Now that you learned the good, the bad and the ugly, you need to know that there are some conditions you must meet as prerequisites before starting your application:

1. You need to be fluent in English - speak, read and write.
2. You have graduated from high school (or hold a GED).
3. You are at least 21 years old.
4. You have a vertical arm reach of 212cm (or 210cm for Etihad Airways) - without shoes, on your tip toes and your height is minimum 160cm (for Emirates only).
5. You have no visible tattoos and no visible piercings while wearing the cabin crew uniform - short sleeve shirts, knee-length skirts.
6. You are physically fit to meet the cabin crew requirements.
7. You can deliver excellent customer service.
8. You have an excellent personal presentation, style, and image.

9.You will be offered a final contract only if you can meet the employment visa requirements (medical exam and background security check).

If you decide this is a lifestyle for you, then let's talk about the future.

1.2 YOUR PROSPECT EMPLOYER

Not all airlines are equal. You will want to know not only who is hiring, but also what is the size of their fleet and human resources, prospects, plans for expansion and hiring, management style, route map and the name of the CEO. These issues will give you a better idea of what you might experience once you are in - not to mention these topics might come up in your final interview. Companies want to know if you were interested enough to research at least the basic information about the airline.

Middle East

There are a couple of big players on the middle-eastern market right now, all of them looking to expand their cabin crew numbers. They are the airlines to join to experience the true expat crew lifestyle. Once hired, they will be taking care of all the paperwork details, such as obtaining a residence visa and work permit, your flight attendant licenses, and exams.

The only language requirement is English, any other language on top of that is considered an advantage.

These airlines create the highest standards of service and in-flight experience for their passengers, and they set the bar quite high for the rest of the airlines in the world.

The average age of flight attendant is quite low, so if you are ambitious and stick around, there are high chances of promotion.

There is no government pension plan; however, your income is tax-free. Be smart and plan ahead for your future.

Europe

Airlines in Europe require that you have the right to live and work in the European Union, as well as fluency in the language of the airline, English and an advantage for speaking any other EU language.

You will not be offered accommodation and transport as you are expected to already reside in that country, have a home and a car.

Obtaining a cabin crew license is sometimes your responsibility and in some countries is a prerequisite for applying for the job.

Being a flight attendant in Europe has enormous benefits, from maternity leave, flexible part-time options, early retirement and good pay.

United States
Airlines in the United States require that you have the right to live and work in the US.
Fluency in English and sometimes Spanish is required. Recent years saw most American airlines cut down massively on their staff and in-flight service. On domestic routes, the passengers may only get a drink and pay for an alcoholic beverage or snack. On most airlines, the passengers need to pay for everything from headsets to the in-flight entertainment system.
You will be expected to not only care for the passenger's safety but also be a good sales person, make inventories of products and manage the on-board financial transactions. The average flight attendant age is quite high, so you need to wait longer to get promoted. A new crew usually starts flying domestic routes with possibilities of promotion to international flights once you gain some experience.
Asia
While the residence visa and flying license might be taken care of by the airline, you will be expected to speak the language of the airline, English and other Asian languages.
There are some competitive airlines in Asia such as Singapore Airlines, Cathay Pacific, Asiana or Hainan Airways.
The average age of the flight attendants is quite low, with some airlines hiring crew as young as 18 years old.

1.3 WHO IS HIRING

All airlines are constantly hiring cabin crew at various frequencies. Some hire every month; others have regular events worldwide or in their hub.
The recruitment events are advertised on each airline's career website, and they can be Open Days, CV Submission Days or Assessment Days.
For the latest recruitment events, you can browse the careers website of each airline.

1.4 YOUR WORRIES AND QUESTIONS ANSWERED

Many of my readers send questions on a daily basis on various topics that ultimately summarize the worries that come up when going for an interview or even just as they start pursuing the thought that this career might be an option. I heard from many people who cannot even bring themselves to go to an Open Day and give it a try for fear of rejection. I am here to shed some light on the common issues that might come into your mind, what can be done, what can't be done and more importantly, what mindset you need to work on.

Scars
Scars can be from chickenpox marks, stitches, cuts or burns.
If you have any marks on your face, neck, arms or legs, you need to see if they can be concealed with make-up, masked by hair or hid under a pantyhose.
If you can do that, the scars should not be a problem.
If you are a man, then you only have to worry about your face and neck, as the uniform consists of a long sleeved shirt and long pants. Men are not allowed to put on make-up while wearing the uniform, so the standards are more rigid here.
Scars can fade in time with laser treatments or by using ointments such as BioOil.

Acne
There are numerous treatments for acne available. See a dermatologist (not a cosmetician or beautician) who will give you prescribed medication for it. If you have scars caused by acne, then see the previous point.

Teeth
Very few people have naturally straight and white teeth. Must you have perfect pearly whites? No! However, teeth are important because the trademark of the flight attendant (or any other person working with customers) is the smile. Your teeth must be clean and without cavities. Even if they are not perfectly straight, if your smile is pleasant and warm, then you should be fine. See your dentist for a cleaning and check-up before the interview.
Crowns, bridges, and implants are all accepted provided they are well kept and look natural if they are visible.
Visible gold teeth and dental tattoos are not allowed.

Braces
Teeth braces are not permitted by the grooming regulations for a flight attendant. You shouldn't wear them for the interview either.

Beauty marks
Beauty marks are brown spots or moles located on your body. You do not need to remove them to become a cabin crew. It is fine and natural to have them.

Tattoos
Tattoos have become very common. However, body art is not appreciated in this industry. If you want to be a flight attendant, you must be ink free in the following areas of your body: arms, legs, neck, face.
Mark on the drawing below the location of your tattoos.
If your tattoos are outside the gray area, you will not be accepted to work as a flight attendant.

You will be asked during your interview to describe the location and size of your tattoos. You might think you can skip this info. You shouldn't. Be truthful, as you will go through a thorough medical check once you are hired. If it is discovered then, you might be sent home.

If you are considering laser removal, make sure you check with your doctor that there will be no visible scar left.

*Some of the airlines will not accept candidates who are having tattoos, regardless if they are visible or not. Make sure to verify the minimum requirements before applying.

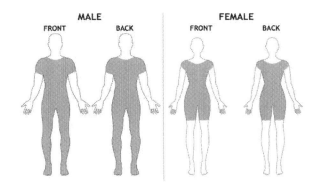

Piercings

The only visible piercings allowed are ear piercings (one in each ear) for ladies. No piercings and jewelry wearing are permitted for men.

If you have piercings in your nose, lip or eyebrows and there is no visible hole when you remove the jewelry, then it is all fine. You must be willing to remove the jewelry from your facial piercings.

If your ears are not pierced, you should not pierce them to get the job. It is not required.

If you have more than one piercing per ear, that is also fine as long as you are not wearing more than one earring.

Height

Most airlines have a minimum height requirement. The reason for this is because they need the cabin crew to be capable of reaching certain safety equipment located in the top compartments of the aircraft. The maximum height where these items are usually stored is the arm-reach required.

For example:

To be considered for Emirates, you must be minimum 160 cm (5"3").

Emirates and Qatar Airways require you to be able to reach 212 cm (6"11") barefoot, on your tip toes.

Etihad Airways only requires an arm-reach of 210 cm (6"10").

You can be 161 cm (5"3") or 180 cm (5"11"), as long as you can reach the 212 cm or 210 cm mark, you will pass this part of the interview.

You can practice by measuring the required height on your wall and mark it with some tape. Some airlines require you to reach it with one hand only, while others want you to reach it with both hands. Practice, stretch and remember that arm reach can be improved with time.

For all the other airlines, the height requirement is mentioned in the minimum requirements on their website. Make sure you check these before applying.

Weight

Am I too fat or too skinny? The airlines require you to have a normal Body Mass Index (BMI). That is a formula that takes into consideration the proportion between your height and weight.

Eye-sight

Even if your vision needs correction, you can apply and pass the medical test if your vision is within the acceptable parameters set by the airline for near and distant visual acuity.

Bear in mind however that for most airlines, you are not permitted to wear glasses. You must be comfortable with the long-term use of contact lenses.

Swimming

One of the minimum requirements is swimming.

For Emirates, Etihad or Qatar Airways, you are expected to be comfortable in the water and swim with the aid of a flotation device. This skill will be practiced during your initial training, where you will learn how to evacuate the aircraft during a ditching situation (emergency landing on water). You will be wearing a life-vest during this exercise.

Beauty

When you say flight attendant, we all think of the model-like girls, tall, skinny with perfect hair and teeth. The misconception here is that all flight attendants must look like that in ordered to get this job. This could not be farther from the truth. If you have a pleasant appearance, relevant experience, speak English and you can make a good impression at the interview, you will be hired even if you do not resemble a Barbie doll.

Education

The only education requirement to apply to be a cabin crew is a high school diploma or a general education diploma (GED).

Everything on top of that is an advantage. It can be either college, university or vocational courses.

You do not need a cabin crew course or an already existing cabin crew license to get the job. All the training will be done in the airline's training academies after you are hired.

Relevant experience

When considering a flight attendant position, relevant experience means any customer experience. That can be work in restaurants, bars, hotels, shops, schools, hospitals, offices or airports. Any work can be translated from a customer service perspective. To see examples, refer to the chapter Creating your CV.

No work experience

If you come straight from school and have absolutely no work experience, but you would like to start a career as a flight attendant, it is possible to do it. Mostly, your interview questions will be based on your school experience or other work you did while in school. To score extra points, include all the organizations you have been involved with, even if they were not paid, such as internships or volunteer work.

If you show during your interview that you are open to learning and willing to become good at what you are doing, you will be hired even if you don't have any experience.

Languages

You must be able to speak, read and write English fluently. This will be observed from how you present your CV, to dialogues during the group exercises, an English test, and the final interview.

All the languages that you speak in addition to English are an advantage.

You are not required to speak Arabic to work for Emirates, Etihad or Qatar Airways.

For any other airlines, check their minimum requirements page.

Age

This is by far the most popular question. The only age requirement for becoming a cabin crew for Emirates, Etihad or Qatar Airways is minimum 21 years old. If you are younger than that, you will have to wait until your 21st birthday.

If you are older than that, it is fine. 27 is not old, 35 is not too old, and even when you are 42, you can become a cabin crew.

"Then why are all the flight attendants so young?" you might ask. The reason is that younger candidates are more likely to prefer this lifestyle: travel, share an apartment, be away from home, have an unpredictable schedule and change the team and the customers you work with all the time. The more you advance in age, the more you are likely to prefer stability, a family and a schedule that will allow the weekends or holidays off.

For the cabin crew position for the airlines in the Middle East, you do have a chance to be hired in your late 20s, early 30s, late 30s and even early 40s. During the interview, you have to demonstrate the ability delivering extraordinary customer service, willingness to learn, adjust, and wisdom to know when to apply your skills and talents. But the most pressing issues for the airlines when considering older candidates are:

How will you be able to cope with the reality that your in-flight manager is probably younger than you? Would you resist or contribute?

Are you physically able to cope with the long hours, irregular schedule and demanding conditions?

How would it feel for you to have a flatmate with the energy, hobbies, and passions of a 21-year-old? How would you get along?

Also, you are much more likely to be hired at an older age if you have relevant experience in the field.

Marital status

You can be a flight attendant if you are married, single, divorced, engaged or in a relationship. In the Middle East, fewer married people are doing this job. And that is because you are moving away from your country, and it is much easier to relocate and find one job instead of two. Also, people who are married prefer to have a regular 9-5 job that will allow them to spend time with their families.

"Why are they not as many married people doing this job?" Because they do not apply for it.

Children

Having children is an amazing experience. You would want to spend as much time as possible with them, and while working as a flight attendant, this will be quite a challenge. You might be away from home for days at a time; you might miss school plays or major milestones. If you want to do this job and have children, then you must have an open mind, a very understanding partner and help either from your parents, in-laws or a hired nanny.

Be aware that kindergarten and school in the Middle East are quite expensive and you will be expected to pay for that yourself, without any assistance from the company.

Also, if you decide to relocate to Dubai, Abu Dhabi or Doha with your family, you will not be able to live with them in the shared company provided accommodation, but find your apartment for which you will be offered a housing allowance from the company. You can apply for the housing allowance only after the first six months of probation.

Nationality

There is no discrimination based on the color of your passport. Airlines in the Middle East cherish the diversity of their crew. If you come from Australia, Mozambique, Peru, Tajikistan, Germany or Philippines, you will be offered the same fair chance to interview for the flight attendant job as any other candidates, and your culture will be celebrated among the other nationalities working for the airline.

How long to wait in between assessment days

- If you participated in an Open Day and your CV was not short-listed, you can go to another Open Day after six months. Remember however that you cannot do the same thing over and over again and expect a different result. When you present the same CV, same photos and the same experience, if you were rejected once, the chances are that you will be rejected the second and the third time as well. Take some time to review your CV, volunteer for some customer service jobs or apply for a new job in the customer service field, learn a new language or acquire a new skill that might benefit you when working as a cabin crew.
- If you participated in an Open Day and your CV was short-listed, but you fail at any point during the assessment day, you will need to wait for six months to participate again in a recruitment event.
- If you passed all stages of the Assessment Day, but you fail the final interview, you will have to wait 12 months before re-applying unless otherwise instructed.
- If you are in any of the situations mentioned above, use the time until you can try again wisely. Reading this book is a great step in your success: being prepared, knowing what to expect and improving yourself to fit the airline's expectations are your keys to get the job.

Confidence and fear of failure

There are a million little reasons to worry about. You can worry about your appearance, about the design of your blouse or small little things you said. Most people are chronic worriers. We analyze every single step we did and go crazy on all the details. Do you believe in the power of the mind? I do, and I believe that you will attract into your life exactly what you have been thinking. If you think you are never good enough and worthy, why would other people think differently? But if you know that you have something to offer and you let people see it by being open, curious, honest and enthusiastic, great accomplishments will be coming your way.

So how do you achieve this inner confidence? Sometimes you might just need to *"fake it till you make it,"* but most of the time it comes naturally when you are well prepared for what is to come.

Think of it like this: the best thing that can happen is getting a job and an amazing new life full of adventure and travels. The worst thing that can happen is a gained experience of how a recruitment day for a reputable international airline looks like. Try to see it all as a learning experience.

You might make it through the CV selection, but fail the group exercise. This is how you learn that your CV is great, but you need to improve your team-working skills.

Or you pass the group exercise but fail the English test. You know exactly what to focus on: improving your English.

You do not need to alter your appearance, buy an expensive suit for the interview or try to pretend to be someone you are not. If you are fit for the job, the job will be a fit for you as well. Otherwise, you will end up being miserable. Do it for passion, and it will not feel like work at all!

You are already perfect. Just let the people around you see that.

CHAPTER 2 - LET'S GET YOU THE JOB

The cabin crew hiring process is called an assessment center or assessment day. Here are some definitions for you:

Assessment Day (or Assessment Center) – Is a process employing multiple techniques and multiple assessors to produce judgments regarding the extent to which a participant displays selected competencies.

Assessor – An individual trained to observe, record, classify and make a reliable judgment about the behaviors of those being assessed.

Exercise (or Task) – A simulation or technique designed to elicit behaviors related to performance requirements of the job.

Your flight attendant skills will be tested in a series of exercises. This hiring method has been adopted by many companies, as a form of interviewing. At the end of the assessment day, you will have a 1-on-1 final interview.

There are three ways of getting to interview for the cabin crew position:

1. Assessment Day - prior to the interview, you will be submitting an online application, sometimes followed by an online video interview. If your application is shortlisted, you will then be called when the airline holds an assessment in your country or city.

2. Open Day - you will participate in the open day that the airlines organize monthly in various countries around the world. If your CV is short-listed, you will then attend an Assessment Day either immediately after, or on a future date which will be communicated to you. No online application is necessary before this event.

3. CV Submission Day - you can drop off your CV and required photographs during the published timings. The shortlisted candidates will be invited to participate in an Assessment Day either the next day or on a future date. No online application is necessary before the event.

We will explore step by step all the options that exist to get you to the assessment day. This chapter is divided into three parts: before, during and after the assessment.

2.1 BEFORE THE ASSESSMENT
2.1.1 CREATING YOUR CV

You need to create a simple, easy to read CV that will set you apart from the other candidates. During Open Days or CV Submission Days, there will be hundreds of people showing up and hoping for a chance. The assessors have only a minute to go through a CV, so you must make sure the relevant information is immediately visible. Think of the assessors as clients in your shop. You have to make sure that your prime merchandise is in the front, attractive and visible.

Even if you have relevant experience, presenting it in a non-attractive manner might diminish your chances of you CV being short-listed for the Assessment Day.

Let's start with what your CV should include.

1. Personal details

Include

✓Full name (First name then family name)

✓Home address (Street, number, city, country)

✓E-mail address (name@mail.com)

✓Telephone number (mobile phone, including the country code)

More personal details will be asked from you when you apply online; however, they are not necessary to be included in the CV.

Do NOT include

✖Date of birth

✖Religion

✖Nationality

✖Marital status

✖Political affiliation

✖Name of your parents

✖Email addresses that contain nicknames such as angel_girl4u@mail.com or me_spiderman1995@mail.com

EXAMPLE

Anna Parker

anna.parker@mail.com

386 Bleecker Street, 10012 New York, NY, U.S.A
+1 946 111 2233

2. Professional experience
In reverse chronological order, start with your latest job.
Include
✓Period you worked at that particular job (month and year)
✓Name of the company and location
✓Job title
✓Job description (in 3-4 bullet points)
✓Outstanding results (if you had any)
Do NOT include
✖the names of your boss
✖salary
✖how many hours per week you worked

If you do not have any professional experience or very limited experience, it is acceptable to start your CV by listing your academic achievements.

See the following list of common jobs and their details to help translate your experience into professional customer service descriptions. For every one of the jobs below, you will find more than 3-4 bullet points. Just choose the ones that are applicable to your experience.

Hostess
- Organize the seating chart and manage reservations.
- Greet guests, escort them to their table and present menus.
- Inform the waiting staff when the customers are seated.
- Ensure cleanliness of the menus, dining room, entryway, and bathrooms.
- Bid farewell to all of the guests.
- Check customer satisfaction.

Waitress
- Escort customers to their tables.
- Present menus to customers, answer questions about menu items and make recommendations upon request.
- Describe and recommend wines.
- Take orders for food and beverages and serve them.
- Prepare and serve specialty dishes as required.

- Check with customers to ensure that they are enjoying their meals and take action to correct any problems.
- Ensure the bill is correct, and the payment is made.

Bartender
- Greet guests, accommodate to their needs and serve them with the utmost respect and professionalism.
- Make customers feel welcome, secure, and relaxed.
- Quickly take a guest's order, prepare the order and complete the transaction in a swift and precise manner.
- Keep work area clean.
- Reinforce a practice of responsible service.
- Maintain a cheerful and upbeat attitude.

Cashier
- Greet and acknowledge every customer.
- Maintain exceptional standards of product knowledge.
- Maintain awareness of all promotions and advertisements.
- Accurately and efficiently ring on registers and maintain all cash and media at the registers.
- Communicate customer requests to management.
- Enter all media from register into the tally program.
- Maintain orderly appearance of register area and supplies stocked.

Shop Assistant
- Be attentive to customers" needs.
- Give information about the features, quality, and availability of different products.
- Help customers find products they are looking for in the shop.
- When necessary, be able to give in-depth technical advice about products.
- Arrange orders and deliveries of stock.
- Advise the customer of information relating to their purchase, such as warranty or product care.
- Make the client aware of any special offers.
- Make sure that all stock is on display.

Sales Assistant
- Assist customers in locating merchandise and answering questions concerning general merchandise.
- Demonstrate use of merchandise upon request.
- Stock shelves, counters or tables with merchandise.

- Process payment following established procedures for different types of transactions.
- Count and balance cash register and receipts.
- Check inventory periodically and place orders with a sales representative.
- Check inventory listing with actual inventory on the shelf and report discrepancies to supervisor.
- Train new sales staff in basic operations and procedures.
- Clean shelves, counters or tables.

Nurse
- Provide direct care and promote comfort to patients.
- Promote healthy lifestyle.
- Interpret medical information to the patient.
- Provide emotional, intellectual and psychologic support.
- Plan, give direction, develop staff and monitor operations.
- Represent both staff and administrations as needed.
- Work together with the doctor.

Fitness Instructor
- Assess the needs and capabilities of individuals through fitness assessment procedures.
- Provide instruction in a variety of fitness activities including non-gym related activities.
- Liaise with doctors, physiotherapists, dietitians and other health professionals to develop fitness programs for clients.
- Help people set and achieve their fitness targets.
- Complete inductions to show people how to use equipment in the gym.
- Supervise use of equipment while making sure that exercise is completed correctly.
- Run group classes.
- Work individually with private clients
- Be informed of developments in health and exercise practice.
- Keep fit.

Spa Therapist
- Provide consistent professional massage and body treatments with spa protocols and accepted certification practices.
- Actively promote the spa and the services available.
- Handle guests" questions and concerns professionally and courteously and provide accurate and immediate responses.

- Provide a level of service which exceeds all guest expectations by completing all treatments in a consistently thorough manner, in the time allocated and by treating all clients with individual attention.
- Attend to the greeting, update records, consultations, refreshments and immediate handling of complaints.
- Ensure all therapist administration is completed at the end of each day (guest records, stock lists and updates of the log book).
- Ensure rooms are kept clean and tidy according to health and safety standards.
- Monitor status of all equipment.
- Restock products in the treatment rooms.
- Participate in ongoing training programs.
- Continually expand the range of treatments qualified to deliver.

(pre)Kindergarten teacher
- Responsible for leading students through creative play and hands-on activities.
- Plan lessons according to the state curriculum and assess students, tailoring their lessons according to the different abilities of children in the classroom.
- Conduct parent-teacher conferences.
- Sponsor after-school clubs or sports teams.
- Plan, set and evaluate grade test, exams, and assignments.
- Supervise student conduct during class and breaks.
- Understand the diverse background students come from, their strength, weakness, and areas of interest.
- Resolve conflict among students by encouraging positive debate.
- Adjust teaching styles to meet individual needs of students.
- Carry out relevant administrative duties.
- Communicate effectively with parents about their children's development.
- Ensuring that the health and safety of children and staff is maintained at all times, both inside and outside the classroom environment.

Hotel Front Desk
- Greet guests with a smile and answer their questions as required.
- Count and verify cash, shift activity, keys and gift certificates with departing shift.
- Print updated in-house, arrival, departure and room status reports.
- Check all unresolved departures.
- Review service requests for arrivals.
- Complete welcome calls.
- Clean and tidy front desk area.
- Work directly with concierge staff.
- Arrange guest travel and transportation (airport transfer, tours, etc).

- Calculate final bills and receive payment.
- Handle direct calls from guests.
- Receive and send emails regarding bookings, reservations or transport.

Secretary/Administrative Assistant/Personal Assistant
- Prepare and manage correspondence, reports, and documents.
- Organize and coordinate meetings, conferences, and travel arrangements.
- Take, type and distribute minutes of meetings.
- Implement and maintain office systems.
- Maintain schedules and calendars.
- Arrange and confirm appointments.
- Organize internal and external events.
- Handle incoming mail and other material.
- Set up and maintain filing systems, work procedures, and databases.
- Communicate in person and/or in writing to answer inquiries and provide information.
- Coordinate the flow of information both internally and externally.
- Operate office equipment.
- Manage office space.

Public Relations Assistant
- Support public relations staff within the organization (advertising and marketing initiatives, scheduled public events and news releases).
- Maintain the executives" schedules, coordinating meetings and travel arrangements, prepare related reports and presentations, create promotional materials, as well as other administrative duties as needed.
- Work closely with account coordinators and account managers to fulfill client needs.
- Actively promote openings and events using press releases and media outlets (print, media, internet).
- Work with individual clients.
- Be involved in the active promotion of the company in social media.

Real Estate Agent
- Provide clients with the best deals on properties while meeting their specific needs.
- Communicate with potential clients to determine what kind of property they are searching.
- Prepare advertisements for open houses and listings and set appointments.
- Prepare properties for sale.

- Serve as a mediator between buyers and sellers.
- Prepare necessary legal documents when an agreement has been made between the two parties.
- Offer guidance to clients about the prices in the market, mortgage aspects, legal procedures and other requirements.

Cabin Crew
- Comply with the airline's safety and emergency procedure.
- Perform onboard equipment checks.
- Provide personalized and graceful service to the guests as underlined in the company's standard service flow.
- Achieve customer service excellence by maintaining open and efficient communication with the passengers.
- Report any concerning matters to the Senior Crew.

EXAMPLE
2008-present   ABC Airline   New York, U.S.A
Cabin Manager
- Supervise a team of 8-14 flight attendants through all stages of the flight.
- Perform onboard coaching and conduct performance management assessments when necessary.
- Ensure the highest level of customer service and satisfaction is achieved on every flight.
- Received 27 letters of commendation from guests and colleagues.

3. Education
List the highest level of education you achieved.
If you went to college, you do not need to mention that you obtained a high school diploma - it is implied.
If you have a master degree, then include your master studies as well as your college in reverse chronological order.
You can also list certification from vocational schools in this section, however, do not include courses that helped you gain skills irrelevant for the cabin crew job such as "computer basics."

Include

✓ dates of attendance

✓ name of the institution, city, and country

✓ degree or certification obtained

Do NOT include

✘your grades and subjects you took
✘your primary or middle school
✘names of your teachers

EXAMPLE
2000-2004 New York University College of Arts and Sciences   New York, U.S.A
Bachelor of Arts (Hons.), major in East-Asian Studies
OR
2000-2004   Millennium High School   New York, U.S.A
High School Diploma

4. Skills
Include a list of competencies that are relevant to the position you are considering. It will be more efficient than a long and overwhelming list. You can always show more during the interview.
Choose 4 or 5 from the following skills. Obviously, mention only the skills you possess.
EXAMPLES
✓Highly adaptable, positive, resilient, open to new ideas.

✓Proven relationship builder with excellent interpersonal skills.

✓A personable individual whose strengths include cultural sensitivity and ability to build rapport with a diverse workforce in a multicultural environment.

✓Dependable, responsible contributor committed to excellence and success.

✓A loyal and dedicated employee with an excellent work record.

✓Energetic personality consistently praised for my passion for work and upbeat, positive attitude.

✓Enthusiastic, knowledge-hungry learner, eager to meet challenges and quickly assimilate new concepts.

✓Fluent in English and ... (insert here your language competencies)

Do NOT include

✘driving license. Your ability to drive a car is irrelevant when applying for a position to work inside a flying airplane.

✘PC use. In this day and age, everybody above 10 and under the age of 50 is computer literate. This is the world we live in.

✘hobbies. This can work against you. The CV is a document to attest to your career history. You want to come across as a professional individual. You do not need the interviewers to know information that is too personal and inappropriate to be brought up in a job interview. It is not what will set you apart. Let the passion for knitting happen outside your job.

5. References
The standard text here is:
"References and letters of appreciation available on request."

When you drop your CV, you may ask the assessors if they require your references list. Have it printed on a separate paper that includes your personal details at the top, and provide it attached to your CV.

The person who is your reference must be your current or previous manager or direct supervisor.

If you don't have any professional experience, list the name of one of your professors who previously agreed to talk about you and your skills with a potential employer.

Include

✓name,

✓title,

✓company or institution,

✓contact email (use the company or university email),

✓contact telephone number.

Do NOT include

✘Your friends, parents or subordinates.

✘Somebody who won't give you best recommendations.

EXAMPLE

John Smith, Sales Manager, ABC Company

john.smith@abc.com

+1 477 321 987

SAMPLE CV

Anna Parker

anna.parker@mail.com
386 Bleecker Street, 10012 New York, NY, U.S.A
+1 946 111 2233

EXPERIENCE

2012-present   ABC Airline   New York, U.S.A
Cabin Crew
- Comply with the airline's safety and emergency procedure.
- Provide personalized and graceful service to the guests as underlined in the company's standard service flow.
- Achieve customer service excellence by maintaining open and efficient communication with the passengers.
- Report any concerning matters to the Senior Crew.

2009-2012   ABC Restaurant   New York, U.S.A
Hostess
- Greet guests, escort them to their table and present menus.
- Inform the waiting staff when the customers are seated.
- Ensure cleanliness of the menus, dining room, entryway, and bathrooms.
- Check customers satisfaction.

EDUCATION

2010-2013
New York University College of Arts and Sciences   New York, U.S.A
Bachelor of Arts, major in East-Asian Studies

SKILLS

✓ Enthusiastic, knowledge-hungry learner, eager to meet challenges and quickly assimilate new concepts
✓ A personable individual whose strengths include cultural sensitivity and ability to build rapport with a diverse workforce in a multicultural environment
✓ A loyal and dedicated employee with an excellent work record
✓ Fluent in English and Japanese, beginner in Mandarin

REFERENCES

References and letters of appreciation available on request.

Important points about your CV

↠Ideally, the CV will be one page long - there is no time for the assessors to read pages and pages of explanations. If you have more than that, cut down your job description to maximum 3-4 bullet points each. The maximum acceptable length is two pages.
↠Keep your language simple and concise.
↠Print two copies of your CV on white paper.
↠Use the spell check. There should be no spelling errors or incorrect sentences. The CV speaks for you.
↠Keep your photo separate, printed on a photo quality paper, do not attach your passport photo next to your name on the CV.
↠Use easy to read fonts such as Verdana, Times New Roman, Helvetica or Arial.

2.1.2 APPLICATION PHOTOS

You will need a full-length photo and a passport photo in digital format for your online application, as well as printed copies for your Assessment Day.

2.1.2.1 Passport photo
Standard passport photo size: 4.5cm x 3.5cm (1.8" x 1.4")
* in the United States the standard passport photo size is 2"x2". You will need to specify the required size of 1.8"x1.4".
Background: white background for Emirates and Etihad, blue background for Qatar Airways. No props.
Digital format: .jpeg, .gif
Printed copies: 8

While taking the photo, look straight ahead and give a genuine smile.

2.1.2.2 Full-length photo
Size: 10cm x 15cm (4" x 6")
Background: white background for Emirates and Etihad, blue background for Qatar Airways. No props.
Digital format: .jpeg, .gif
Printed copies: 4
***Emirates will require for the Final Interview one full-length business attire photo and two full-length casual photos. Provide casual photos suitable for an employee to see. Do not show pictures of you drinking or smoking, in a bathing suit (or any other revealing clothing) or in compromising circumstances.

POSING
Smile.
Face the camera with a good posture.
Ensure both legs are visible. Do not cross them over.
Both arms and hands should be visible on the sides of the body.

LADIES
What to wear?

- ✓A power skirt-suit in black, brown, gray, dark blue or dark green. Make sure it is fitted (not loose).
- ✓A blouse or collared shirt, preferably white.
- ✓The skirt must not be shorter than knee length.
- ✓High heel shoes (court shoes) without ankle straps in a dark color complementing the suit.
- ✓Skin colored stockings.

What NOT to wear
- ✖ scarfs
- ✖ jeans
- ✖ mini-skirts
- ✖ colored pantyhose such as black, red, purple or yellow
- ✖ floral patterns
- ✖ revealing clothing
- ✖ T-Shirts
- ✖ sandals
- ✖ open toe shoes
- ✖ bathing suits
- ✖ national costumes
- ✖ sunglasses
- ✖ hats
- ✖ musical instruments
- ✖ plastic, colored or big jewelry
- ✖ mobile phone
- ✖ handbag

Make-up, hair, and accessories
- ✓If your hair is longer than shoulder-length, it should be tied in a bun and any loose hairs secured in place with hair spray.
- ✓If your hair is short, style it nice and neat.
- ✓Wear make-up. You should choose foundation, eye shadow, mascara and lipstick matching your skin tone. Do not put too much.
- ✓If you choose to wear jewelry, keep it conservative - wedding/engagement ring, pearl or diamond stud earrings, an understated necklace, and a small watch.

This is how you should present yourself in your full-length business attire photograph.

HOW TO BECOME A FLIGHT ATTENDANT

GENTLEMEN
What to wear?

✓A suit in black, brown, gray, dark blue or dark green, simple or with pinstripes.

✓A collared, long sleeved and preferably white shirt.

✓A neck tie that is complementing the suit and the shirt.

✓Dark color polished shoes.

What NOT to wear
✖ jeans
✖ suit in light or pastel colors such as blue, yellow or white
✖ white shoes
✖ jacket over the shoulder
✖ shorts
✖ open shirts
✖ T-Shirts
✖ sandals
✖ national costumes
✖ sunglasses
✖ hats
✖ musical instruments
✖ jewelry
✖ make-up
✖ mustaches, goatees or beards

✖ mobile phone
✖ briefcase

Hair and accessories

✓Hair should be short and neatly groomed. Do not shave it all off.

✓Show a clean, shaved face.

✓The only accessories you should wear are your wedding ring and a watch.

This is how you should present yourself in your full-length business attire photograph.

Important points about your photographs

↦Take both the passport photos and the business attire full-length pictures at the same time.

↦If you can afford it, go to a professional studio to have these photographs taken. The investment will pay for itself.

↦Make sure you smile and look like a flight attendant already.

↦These photographs will speak for you when you are not around: they will be presented, together with your CV and the notes of your performance on the assessment day, to the HR Department of the airline. After the viewing of the above mentioned, a decision will be made regarding your offer of employment. Present your best.

2.1.3 ONLINE APPLICATION

Going online on the career website of the airline, you will complete an online application. This is an online creation of your CV and it will be referred to from the interview until the moment you join the airline.

2.1.4 ONLINE VIDEO INTERVIEW

Not all airlines use the online video interview as part of their selection process, but some of them do (such as Emirates and Fly Dubai). This is a new technique employed to assess the candidates applying online, before the one-on-one interaction with a recruiter on the Assessment Day.

As you are creating your online profile on the airline's careers page, one of the steps is "online video interview."

When preparing for this stage, focus on planning the answers for the questions you will receive (most of them behavioral questions similar to the ones you will receive during the final interview, sample questions and sample answers can be found in the Chapter "101 Questions and Answers for the Final Interview").

Your appearance in front of the camera should be spotless - dress as you would for a face-to-face interview, with business attire, hair arranged and makeup done (for ladies).

Being nervous is normal.

The video interview will involve answering a few questions about yourself. The number of questions you receive is different for each airline; however, this step should not take more than 15-20 minutes to complete. The online video interview should be completed in one sitting, but you will have the opportunity to practice first.

This stage is used to assess your conversational English skills, as well as your relevant experience, paired with the ability to make a good first impression. So the way you present yourself during this stage is crucial. Use Chapter 2.2.1, "How to dress for your assessment day," to guide you in ensuring your appearance matches the job expectations.

To be prepared for this, test yourself by recording your answers to the "101 Questions and Answers for the Final Interview" (Chapter 2.2.7.2) on your phone or computer. Review them, ask a friend or colleague to offer feedback and adjust what needs adjustment.

You won't need special equipment to complete this step, such as a video camera or a recording studio. You will only need a device equipped with internet connection and a video camera (tablet, mobile phone or computer).

Important points about your online application

↠Fill in every single field, paying extra attention to the ones marked with a star

↠Do not close the window until you complete all the steps.

↠Be prepared to answer the unique questions each airline asks about your motivation to become a cabin crew, the reason for choosing a particular airline and examples from your customer service experience.

↠You can come back to update your application, but it is more efficient to do it all at one time.

↠Don't let your ambition to achieve perfection in the online application stage stand in your way of actually applying for the job. Prepare as much as possible, but in the end, click on the 'submit Application," not matter how nervous you are.

↠The airline usually takes six weeks to review applications. You can regularly check the status of your application on the online portal.

↠If you have been shortlisted, you will receive an email with the next steps.

↠If you haven"t been shortlisted, you may not receive a personalized email, but your online status will change to "not shortlisted" or "unsuccessful."

↠If you have no update on your application after six weeks, you should assume you have not been successful at this time.

2.2 THE ASSESSMENT
2.2.1 HOW TO DRESS FOR YOUR ASSESSMENT DAY

The simplest and best advice is to dress like a flight attendant already. Formal business attire is the standard requirement that the airline gives for the day of the interview. What does that mean? It is quite a vague instruction. Below you will find an explanation of what a business attire is for female and male candidates.

LADIES

1. Suit
Choose a fitted suit in a dark color. It can be black, gray or navy.
It is highly recommended you wear a skirt. The length should not be above the knee. Most middle-eastern airlines favor a modest and conservative style, and so should you. The jacket should be fitted and classic-elegant.

2. Shirt
Go for a simple, collared shirt. Nothing says business more than a clean, crisp shirt. Do not show cleavage.

3. Scarf
This is the patent "fight attendant detail" on a business attire. While you are not allowed to wear a scarf for your application photos or final interview, you can wear one during the Open Day. This is finally an area where you can play with color. Go for red, green or purple. Your image will stick longer with the interviewer.

4. Pantyhose
Choose a skin-colored, simple model. Do not wear colored stockings, patterns or fishnet designs.

5. Shoes
Should be a dark color, closed pattern. Go for classic and comfortable rather than fashion. Simple, black, high or mid heel are the best. No platforms, peep-toe stilettos or flat shoes. Wearing a bit of heel will give you a more confident stroll. Keep in mind though that it will be a very long day.

6. Make-up
Use simple, neutral colors such as brown and gray eyeshadow, mascara, blush, and lipstick. To score extra points, look for pictures of the flight attendants, and copy their make up. Make it easy for your interviewer to already imagine you in their uniform. Carry your make up pouch with you and reapply throughout the day

7. Hair
If you have long hair, tie it back in a simple bun. If your hair is short, comb it back and secure it with some gel or hairspray. Do not opt for a spiky just-out-of-the-bed look. Once again, pretend you already have the job.

8. Nails

The biggest winner in this category is a natural manicure, light pink or beige. Avoid dark unnatural strong colors such as electric blue, purple or black.

9. Perfume

Use subtle perfume, nothing too intense.

10. Jewelry

Keep it simple with maximum two rings and modest size earrings. Diamond-like studs or pearls are the best options. If you choose to wear a necklace, go for classic styles in silver or gold or a set of pearls.

Do not wear bracelets, as they can make noise while you are writing your exercises. Always wear a watch in a classic style with metal, black, brown or white bracelet.

11. Handbag

Wear a purse in simple leather that matches your shoes and suit. Have the following items with you:
- make-up pouch and a small mirror
- nail polish
- spare pantyhose
- tissues
- hairbrush, hair pins and hair spray
- water & snacks
- mints or other breath fresheners (no chewing gum)
- pens and a notebook
- money
- mobile phone on silent mode
- documents
- printed copy of 101 Questions and Answers for the Final Interview.

This is how you should present yourself on your cabin crew recruitment day

GENTLEMEN

1. Suit

Choose a suit in a dark color. It can be black, gray, dark green or navy. If you do not have a suit (jacket and pants made from the same material), then opt for similar or complementing colors for your jacket and trousers. You could have a black jacket and dark gray pants or a beige (light brown) jacket and brown pants. If you do not own a suit, check with your local wedding planners. You can always rent one for the day.

2. Shirt

A simple, long sleeved, buttoned shirt matching the suit color. The safest choice is a white shirt.

3. Tie

Whenever you go for a job interview, you must wear a tie. Choose one to complement your suit, shirt and complexion. If you do not want to play with color, choose a tie in the same color as your suit. A black suit with a white shirt and black tie. Avoid leather ties or funny drawings.

4. Socks

Opt for socks in a dark color, matching the rest of your outfit. You should not wear white socks or funky socks with cartoons or bright colors.

5. Shoes

Choose a dark color, with or without laces. Make sure they are clean and polished.

6. Make-up

Do not wear any!

7. Hair

If you have long hair, it is time to cut it. Your hair should be short, but not fully shaved and well groomed. Your facial hair should be removed. A clean, shaved complexion should be displayed. No mustaches, goatees or 1-day beards.

8. Nails

Cut them short.

9. Accessories

Do not wear bracelets, necklaces outside your shirt, earrings or any other rings except a wedding band (if you are married). Always wear a watch in a classic style with metal or leather straps. Avoid the big plastic watches.

10. Perfume

Do not use too much or anything too strong.

11. Briefcase

You should have a briefcase, laptop bag or a backpack with you containing some items you might need during the day:
- tissues
- comb
- water and snacks

- pens and a notebook
- money
- mobile phone on silent mode
- documents
- printed copy of the 101 Question and Answers for the Final Interview

This is how you should present yourself on your cabin crew recruitment day.

2.2.2 HOW TO BE CONFIDENT DURING THE ASSESSMENT DAY

Feeling nervous during the assessment day is normal. Many candidates worry about showing their nervousness. You should not think about this too much. Once you are in the room and the process starts rolling, you will forget about it and be yourself.

Showing nervousness is also an indicative that you care about the job and the assessment day is important to you. The recruiters understand this.

Real confidence comes from having the following combo: preparation, positive inner dialogue and positive body language.

Preparation means knowing what to expect and more importantly, knowing what is expected from you: how to prepare your CV and photos, how to dress for the interview, what to say and how to react. You are perfecting this by reading this book right now.

Positive inner dialogue, however, is something most people struggle with. Statements such as "*I am not good enough to get job!*", "*Who am I to dream so big?*", "*How dare I think I am worthy?*", "*I simply can't imagine being allowed to travel the world when I was born in...,*" are present in our heads. Self-doubt used to be healthy. From the evolutionary perspective, we needed it to limit ourselves so we can stay safe: "*I

am not big enough to fight that bear!" or "I can't travel because it is safer to stay in this cave with my family." In the modern day, the inner dialogue is based on unachievable standards of beauty, wealth, and perfection and fueled by social media polished feeds and how we have been talked to as children.
So how to rise above the mental chatter that slows down achieving success?

Wear something that makes you feel beautiful
We tend to behave more confidently when we feel good about our appearance. So do you best when choosing your interview outfit. It does need to be a formal business attire, but that is the only limitation. You are free to experiment with the rest. When you put this outfit on, it should be an instant mood lifter.

Do your best then let go
Obsessing over the tiny details after the event has passed is counter-productive, yet it is what most people do. Instead, consider coming up with a plan about the exact steps to take so you can feel you did your absolute best during the day: great CV, beautiful photos, catchy and relevant introduction, helpful attitude. Vow to yourself to perform like this during the assessment day. Once the day is over, go through what happened during the day. Make a note (a real one, on paper) about what you did, what you could have done better and what you were very proud of. Then let go. Mentally and emotionally, there is nothing really that you can still do. The part where you had to show up and do your best has passed. The outcome is not something you can control.

"It's funny how some distance
Makes everything seem small,
And the fears that once controlled me
Can't get to me at all!"

My four-year-old daughter was singing it as I was working on this book (it's the soundtrack of Frozen) and I think everybody should be singing it with all they might have every day!

Imagine the interviewer when they were just like you
During the job interview, it seems that the person conducting the assessment is holding the absolute power over your future. And so we get intimidated by their presence and can't perform as good as we know we can. We say silly things, tremble, forget all the English we once mastered and feel completely and utterly small.
So here is a little **exercise** to help with the nerves:
When waiting in line to hand over the CV, or listening to the company presentation, look at the interviewer and imagine them years ago when they were just like you: a hopeful candidate waiting in line to hand over their CV and become cabin crew. How they must have felt, their nervousness and profound desire to succeed. Just like you. Just like to candidate sitting next to you.
Then get your mind back to your day. You will be okay.

Use positive affirmations
To produce positive thoughts, we need to start by verbalizing them. If they don't come naturally, we just need to schedule them. Like a chore.
Say these things out loud, to yourself or a crowd.
Repeat as often as possible, at least couple of times every day.
Say:
I will be a flight attendant
I am beautiful.
My smile helps people.
This lifestyle is a perfect match for who I want to become.
The world is my school. Learning never ends.
I am good. I do good.
I am a citizen of the world.
I am smart.
I deserve a good life.
Visualize your success
Sit down, close your eyes and create a movie of how the interview will go. How you will walk into the room, participate in the tasks, smile and chat with your colleagues. Then imagine the end of the interview followed by the golden call. Visualize packing for your relocation, arriving at your new home, wearing the uniform, serving people, going to Paris, Tokyo and Rio. Go deep into it. See yourself succeeding. Allow yourself to dream. Play this movie in your head every day until it becomes your reality.
Positive body language
Embracing this is what will also help you be more confident by being aware of the signals that you send and the message they convey.
Body language is a form of non-verbal communication. It consists of facial expressions, body posture, gestures and eye movements. Humans send and interpret all these signs almost entirely subconsciously. Understanding the importance of things you do not say puts you one step ahead during the assessment process.
Body language makes up for more than 90% of our communication, and it takes only 30 seconds for somebody to decide if they like us or not.
I am sure you have been in a situation when you talked to someone, and you knew that what they said was very different from what they meant. All by getting clues from their body language.
To ensure that you make the biggest impact when meeting someone now, keep in mind the following aspects:
Facial expressions
The smile is the most important feature of flight attendants. They are always smiling and looking happy. They make their passengers feel welcomed and at ease.

When you are dropping your CV, talking to your interviewer and colleagues during the tasks or breaks, keep positive facial expressions. Smile and say, *"Thank you!"* often.

Ask your family and close friends if they noticed any facial ticks you might have: lifting your eyebrow when you are bored or questioning, pursing your lips when avoiding the truth, rolling your eyes when disagreeing or looking down when you feel intimidated.

Body posture

When seated, keep your spine straight and upright, your hands resting on the table or your lap.

Sitting far in your seat with your legs parted or arms in the air can be interpreted as boredom or an attitude of superiority.

When you go through the 1-on-1 final interview, the easiest way to deal with sending the right signal is to mirror the assessor's body posture.

Eye contact

Always maintain eye contact with the people talking to you. The easiest way to do this without looking weird is to focus on the point located between the eyebrows of the person in front of you.

If you get tired, move your gaze to the person's left ear, then right ear.

Do not look up or down; this may signify boredom or avoiding to answer truthfully.

Gestures

In stressful situations, we tend to fold our hands across our body because it makes us feel more protected. Avoid doing this during the job interview, as it may be perceived as defensive.

Support your words with open hand gestures. When introducing a colleague to the rest of the group you may point with both hands towards the person.

Subconscious gestures such as touching your mouth, ears or nose may betray what you think. Most people touch their mouth after they say a lie or their ears after they heard something they do not like.

Be aware of what you do with your hands.

Being confident is truly important. It will make you or break you when applying to become a cabin crew. Finding the right balance between being humble and self-assured is a talent worth pursuing. Start working on your confidence just as much as you work on your English test, group exercise or CV. It is in the end, just an exercise. I want to end this chapter with my favorite quote:

> "Attitude is more important than facts. It is more important than the past, than education, money, circumstances, than failure and success, than what other people think, say, or do. It is more important than appearance, ability, or skill. It will make or break a business, a home, a friendship, an organization...

> The remarkable thing is I have a choice every day of what my attitude will be. I cannot change my past. I cannot change the actions of others. I cannot change the inevitable. The only thing I can change is attitude.
> Life is ten percent what happens to me and ninety percent how I react to it."
> -Chuck Swindoll

2.2.3 DOCUMENTS

Thinking ahead and being optimistic that your CV will be selected, you should already prepare some documents for the final stages of the interview.
Make sure you have ready the following:
CV - 2 copies on white paper
reference list - 2 copies on white paper
copy of your passport first page - 2 colored copies of the first page (the page with the photo and your personal details)
a copy of your highest educational certificate plus all the other extra certificates you have (certified language skills or other relevant vocational courses)
service letters - from the current and previous employer
passport photos - 6
full-length photo in business attire - 1

2.2.4 OPEN DAY

Numerous airlines organize Open Days as recruitment events.
This is the definition is given by Emirates:
"Open Days are information sessions held all over the world to give you the opportunity to find out what it's like to work as Emirates Cabin Crew. These sessions are also an opportunity for you to meet our recruitment team, submit your CV and begin the process of starting your new career with Emirates. If you've got what it takes, you'll be invited to attend the Emirates Cabin Crew screening and assessment process, either the same day or the following day, depending on the number of candidates in attendance. Final interviews will be scheduled over the course of the same week. It is a very good idea, therefore, to plan ahead and have copies of your documents and certificates ready and available."
Etihad says: *"an Open-Assessment is open to anyone who meets our criteria, an invitation to attend is not necessary."*

Bear in mind that even when you apply online, and you receive an invitation from the airline to participate in an Open Day, it is not guaranteed that your CV will be selected and you will be offered a chance to participate in the assessment day.

What is an Open Day?

The Open Day is a recruitment event you can attend without previously applying online. That means that you can just show up at the advertised location with the required documents and hope that your CV is selected and you will be asked to stay longer and participate in the Assessment Day.

What will happen during the Open Day?

When you arrive at the location, you can be overwhelmed by the number of people who showed up. There have been instances where more than 500 people wanted to participate in the Open Day.

You will be asked into a conference room and shown a video about the airline and the city where the airline is based. It should not take more than 20 minutes, followed by a Questions and Answers session. You can ask the recruiters anything you like about the airline, its employees, its base, life in the Middle East or career perspective with the airline.

Don't be shy and if you have a good question that might benefit the others, ask.

Pay attention during the presentation and do not ask about details already covered in the video.

Questions you can ask

✓Is there a maximum age practiced by your airline for hiring flight attendants?

✓What is the process for in-house promotions?

✓What is the airline policy regarding family members visiting?

✓What is the best part of being a flight attendant?

✓How does the airline support continuous education?

Questions you should NOT ask

✘What are my chances to meet a nice guy in the first class and get married?

✘Do you have rude passengers? Is this a difficult job?

✘Do we have to clean the toilets?

✘Is it true that during night flights we are not allowed to sleep or read magazines?

After the Q&A session, you will be invited to drop your CV and your photos. You will be asked 2-3 questions about what the assessor finds interesting in your CV.

This is your first impression with the recruiter. Smile and be polite, answer the questions truthfully without losing yourself into too many details.

At this point, you will be given a number that will be your reference number for the remaining of the assessment process.

CV

Printed on white paper, ideally, will have only one page and a separate page with references. While you hand in your resume, ask if they require the details of your references and attach the separate paper to the main page. You should have a paper clip in your bag.

Photos
One full length colored photograph
Four colored passport size photographs

There will be two scenarios here:
- If more than 100 people show up, the assessors will need extra time to go through all the CVs. You would be asked at this point to go home and expect a phone call in the afternoon if your CV was selected. This is when you will be informed of the details of the Assessment Day. Most of the time it is scheduled for the next day.
- If there aren"t so many candidates (less than 100 people), you will be asked to go for a coffee break while the assessors look through the CVs and select the ones who will be participating in the Assessment Day.

If you are not from the city where the Assessment Day takes place, think ahead and make arrangements for accommodation and transportation. The Assessment Day will last one full day, and the Final Interview will be held the following day.

2.2.5 CV SUBMISSION DAY

You can recognize this type of event by the time frame for submitting your documents at the location: "anytime between xx AM and xx PM."
Locations and timings will be provided on airline's careers website. You are expected to go to the published venue anytime during the set schedule with the documents required by the airline.
The standard documents are:
- **CV**
- **passport photo**
- **Full-length photo**
- **a copy of your passport** (Qatar Airways only)
- **the copy of your highest educational certificate** (Qatar Airways only)

You are expected to present yourself in the same way you would for the assessment day - wear business attire, smile and answer the questions the assessors will ask you.

2.2.6 ASSESSMENT DAY

Assessment Days are organized in certain countries, and the date of the event will be advertised by the airline on their career website. To participate in the Assessment Day, you will need to register online, create an application and wait for your application to be processed by the airline's HR Department.

For some airlines, the shortlisted candidates will be asked to participate in an online video interview.

Only the successful candidates are then invited to the Assessment Day.

Recruitment Agency

In some countries, the initial selection process is organized before the assessment day by using a local recruitment agency. You will find this information on the airline's careers website.

At the agency you will be required to fill-in application papers, complete an English test and a pre-interview session.

You should go to the agency as if you were going for the interview with the airline. They hold the decision to offer you a chance to participate in the Assessment Day with the airline, so you must be flawless in your presentation.

You will be asked to fill in an application form with your personal details and attach a copy of your CV. Most agencies have a standard CV format which will be created with the data you provide.

Next step is a basic English test where you will be asked to translate an aviation related text and also show your capability of having a short conversation in English with the representative.

If you are not sure of aviation-related terms, translate in advance the following words in your native language:

aircraft
airport
seat belts
seat belt sign
safety measures
non-smoking
lavatory
take-off
landing
departure
arrival
turbulence
weather conditions
captain

cabin crew
ground staff
After the English test, you will have a pre-interview session with one of the recruitment representatives from the agency.
Your experience, education, and motivation to become a flight attendant will be discussed.
Be prepared and make a good first impression.
Once the initial screening is completed, you will be given the details and the invitation to the Assessment Day.
The airline pays the recruitment agency to assist them in finding the right candidates for the cabin crew position. You should not be asked to pay the agency for finding you work. If that is the case, you should contact the airline immediately. You might be the victim of a scam. All the official partner agencies are advertised on the online career pages of the airline. If the information is not published by the airline, it is very likely the agency is not an official partner and has no authority in pre-screening candidates.
If your country doesn"t organize the Assessment Day in conjunction with a recruitment agency, you can just proceed to apply online on the airline career's page.

The Assessment

New Oxford American Dictionary gives us the following definition of the word:
Assessment [noun]
The evaluation or estimation of the nature, quality, or ability of someone or something
A teacher's assessment of the student's abilities: evaluation, judgment, rating, estimation, appraisal, analysis, opinion.
Another useful definition:
An assessment center is a process used in the selection of qualified individuals for a job or role in an organization. It employs a variety of techniques and multiple observers in a closed setting to evaluate candidates. Based on an analysis of the skills and competencies for the job in question exercises for the candidates are selected to reveal information regarding the required qualities and attributes.
The airlines' Assessment Day is an Assessment Center type of recruitment. Throughout the day you will participate in various tasks and exercises, each meant to establish if you are a good candidate for the cabin crew position.
After each exercise, the airline representatives will select the candidates who will go through to the next stage.
At the end of each exercise, you will be handed a piece of paper with your reference number on it. The paper will say either
Congratulations, you have been successful... or
Thank you for participating in the Assessment Center. We regret to inform you...
Let's make sure that the only paper you see is the first one.

HOW TO BECOME A FLIGHT ATTENDANT

2.2.6.1 INTRODUCTION

Introduce yourself

You will be asked to say a couple of words about yourself. Sometimes you will be asked to say something about yourself other people will not know just by looking at you.

Be original and say something that will stick in the memory of the recruiters. Cover only professional aspects. You don't want to shock anybody at this point.

For example, you can say:

"Hello everybody, my name is Anna. I am currently working at ABC Stores as a sales assistant. Previously I worked at XYZ Office as a personal assistant. I graduated last year with a BA from the University of NY. You probably wouldn't guess that all my books are alphabetically arranged."

You kept it professional but light and breezy and revealed a personal aspect that implies that you are an organized person.

Introduce others

You might be asked to sit at a table with 5-8 other people and introduce the person sitting next to you. This can be achieved by asking open-ended questions to the other person, such as:

What is your name?
How old are you?
Where do you come from?
What is your career background?
What is your educational background?
What was the last place you visited?
What is your favorite food?
Tell me something funny about yourself.

Make the presentation not more than 4-5 sentences, use open body gestures, use the person's name often and smile. Address the other people sitting at the table, not the assessor.

2.2.6.2 REACH TEST

This is a non-negotiable aspect of the selection process. At the assessment for Emirates and Qatar Airways, you will need to reach 212 cm on your tip toes. When applying for Etihad the required arm reach is 210 cm.

For Emirates, there is as well a minimum height requirement and this will be checked at this point as well.

Why the rule?
There is a lot of safety equipment located in the upper areas of the aircraft, in storage compartments. You need to be able to reach those. Also, you will need to close the passenger's overhead bins or reach the containers store in the galley (kitchen).
212 cm (or 210 cm) is the maximum height where the equipment is located.
When you have an emergency landing, or you have to take off in 5 minutes, you cannot ask a colleague to reach it for you.
The good news is that with practice, your arm-reach can improve considerably, sometimes even with 2 or 3 cm.
Practice by measuring 212 or 210 cm and put a tape mark on your wall. If you are short, practice every day to reach the mark. You will get better and better at it. Practicing yoga also helps with your flexibility.
You will be asked to reach the mark on the wall with one hand. If you have a hard time doing it or you are just at the limit, the assessors might ask you to reach the mark with both hands.
You can be on your tip toes and stretch as much as you can to reach it.
The first round of eliminations happens at this stage. People who made a good first impression and can reach the height mark will be offered to stay for the next round.

Important points about the first stage of the assessment day
↳Get to the location early (at least 30-45 minutes before the set time) and get to know the people you will be spending your day with.
↳Be friendly with everybody. Do not sit shy in a corner. Try to start a conversation with ice-breakers such as *"I love your shoes!"*, *"Your lipstick fits you perfectly, where did you get it from?"* or *"Hi, my name is ...."*
↳Smile and be polite.
↳Do not attempt to shake hands with the interviewer unless they initiate it.
↳ Participate in all tasks enthusiastically, but without becoming the center of attention.

2.2.6.3 THE GROUP EXERCISE

Keep in mind the position you are interviewing for.
The ideal flight attendant is not a leader, nor a follower, but rather somebody who will take charge when the situation requires it and step back when necessary. But above all, a cabin crew must be an excellent team member all the time.

The perfect candidate will be able to understand that aviation rules concerning the safety and security of the aircraft, crew, and passengers, are rules that are not discussed or negotiated; they are to be followed at all times.

A successful candidate will also be able to show an open mind, flexibility and a can-do attitude.

This is the reason why we have a group exercise in place. A game is a fun way to see how people react truthfully. Some people come to the assessment with the thought that they can hide who they are and become the model of cabin crew they think the airline wants. Most likely, they will not be able to hold their act together for the full day. People will show their true colors quickly during the group exercise.

The exercise is usually a scenario given to your group to brainstorm, a task to fulfill, a complaint to solve or construction to build. We will go one by one through every one of these examples. However, there is one critical aspect to keep in mind: **The result of the task is irrelevant!** This may come as a shock, but there are other, more important issues that are observed during your exercise:

How you co-operate with others?
How do you express your concerns if you have any?
What is your conflict style?
How do you agree and how do you disagree?
Are you a leader or a follower?
Are you enthusiastic or rather just sit quietly and let others be in charge?
How do you prioritize?
In the case of role play, how do you hold your emotions together in a highly stressful scenario?

And yes, it is possible to establish all of the above just by observing you and your group mates build a tower with Lego. Do not forget that it is just a game, so do not take the game content too seriously!

2.2.6.3.1 EXERCISE 1 - CUSTOMER SERVICE SCENARIOS AND ROLE PLAY

HIGHLIGHTS

This is an exercise in which the following capabilities are assessed:
- empathizing with the customer
- clear and straightforward verbal communication
- active listening
- assertiveness
- offering creative and efficient solutions to a practical issue
- explaining a personal point of view in a simple and concise manner

- negotiation
- working as a part of the group
- accepting opinions from other team members
- agreeing and disagreeing in a constructive manner
- respecting the set timing
- keeping calm and composed when dealing with a stressful scenario

SCENARIO 1

Mr. John Smith is your passenger from London to Dubai. During the meal service, he refuses the food, and he doesn"t want to accept anything that you offer him.

After the service, you offer Mr. Smith some water and ask if there is anything you can do to serve him. You find out that he is upset because he was downgraded from Business Class to Economy Class due to overbooking. He is displeased with how the airline dealt with this, and he is thinking to switch his return flight to another carrier.

The team should come up with a solution for Mr. Smith's distress. At the end of your debate, one member will be nominated to role-play the scenario.

You have 20 minutes to complete the exercise.

HOW TO HANDLE THE EXERCISE

For this exercise, the correct approach requires you to display your customer service and problem-solving skills, while working harmoniously with your team members.

LANGUAGE TO USE

Guide yourself from the following examples as to the type of language to use:

When expressing an opinion

I believe we should consider first what resources we have in the aircraft to solve the customer's issue. What do you think?

When not agreeing with a team member

I can see how giving him an upgrade to First Class might solve the problem, but I believe we do not have the authority to do that. The ground staff would have done it themselves if it was an option.

When keeping the time

I just want to remind you that we have 5 minutes left.

When making a group decision, if you are the one writing

So we agreed that as a first approach, we would listen as much as possible to what the customer has to say, is this correct?

SAMPLE ANSWER

The group has decided that the most important part of handling this issue is empathy. We will encourage Mr. Smith to open up and tell us about his experience and how he felt about it. Then we will ask him for a solution. What does he want us to do to make up a little bit for what happened to him?

At this point, Mr. Smith might be happy just because he has been heard, or he will give us an alternative. If his request is reasonable, such as a big bottle of water, or a night kit with earplugs and an eye mask from Business Class, then we will fulfill it. If the request is not reasonable, such as asking to be upgraded to First Class, then we will explain that it is not within our means to fulfill his wish.

If Mr. Smith does not want to give us a solution, then we will suggest a glass of champagne, a big bottle of water or reseating to another area in Economy Class with more leg room.

Of course, we will ask if that is an acceptable solution.

When an agreement has been made, we will check back regularly with Mr. Smith.

We will inform the Purser for proper documentation of the incident, and the ground staff at the arrival airport to offer Mr. Smith extra care during his transit.

TIPS FOR THE ROLE PLAY

↪The assessor will nominate one candidate to play the role of the cabin crew, while she will play the role of the customer.

↪Expect the "customer" to display strong negative emotions such as anger or disappointment. Stay calm and allow them to talk and explain how they feel. Don't take it personally.

↪Feeling nervous is normal. Not only is this your cabin crew interview, but it is also a highly stressful potential scenario to deal with.

↪Be polite and try to keep your emotions in check.

↪Formulate an opening statement, as well as a closing statement. It can be: "Mr. Smith, I can't imagine how you must feel. I would like to make this better for you. Please tell me how." To conclude the talk, say something along these lines: "Mr. Smith, thank you for allowing me to address this issue. I hope I managed to improve your experience with our airline."

↪Decide in advance what you are offering. Have 2-3 options.

↪Expect the customer to deny at least one of your suggestions.

↪Practice as much as you can before the actual scenario. You can do so by yourself, in the mirror, recording yourself on video or ask a friend to play the role of the angry customer. The more you practice, the less likely you are to be surprised by the attitude of the customer.

SCENARIO 2

You are the front-desk manager in a five-star hotel. The hotel has been overbooked. You only have two rooms left. From the list of customers below, decide who will get the rooms and what alternatives you will present the other guests.

-Platinum customer, who has been a guest in your hotel for the past five years, staying on average one week every month. He knows you and your staff by name.

-The daughter of the Ministry of Tourism, in transit for her early morning flight to Miami.

-A business woman attending a conference in the city

-Elderly couple. The lady had a minor surgery six months before the trip. They are due for a four-night stay.
-A party-loving socialite who has over 100.000 Instagram followers.
-Famous travel blogger who came to town specifically to review the hotel.
-The general manager of a sister hotel in a different state. This is a business trip supported by the hotel corporation. He is not paying for the room.
-Five months pregnant woman who is traveling with her 2-year-old daughter. She is exhausted and asked for a suite or connecting room.

At the end of your debate, one member will be nominated to present your solution.

After the presentation, you will be randomly nominated to role-play the front-desk manager in different customer scenarios.

You have 20 minutes to decide which customers will get the rooms.

HOW TO HANDLE THE EXERCISE

Regardless of the circumstances, there is no easy way to communicate a disappointing outcome or situation to a customer. No people deserve more than others to be turned down. Discussing the ethical approach to this scenario is a waste of valuable time for your team.

Your focus should be on delivering the bad news with respect and empathy towards the customer and in the same time offer acceptable alternatives.

If you are not limited by the scenario, extravagant alternatives are acceptable, and you should use your imagination to find these.

LANGUAGE TO USE

Guide yourself from the following examples as to the type of language to use:

When expressing an opinion

I believe we should consider first what is the worst case scenario for each customer. For example, the socialite might post a negative comment on social media. It would be bad press that has the potential of going viral. What do you think?

When not agreeing with a team member

I can see how giving the room to the pregnant woman might be an ethical option, but wouldn't you say that offering her another hotel option plus complimentary nanny service would be a more valuable experience for her?

When keeping the time

I just want to remind you that we have 10 minutes left.

When making a group decision, if you are the one writing

So we agreed that we would give the first room to the platinum customer, correct?

SAMPLE ANSWERS

Platinum Guest - We will offer one room to him. Our 5-year business relationship with him is personal and valuable. The worst case scenario is that he will move his business to another hotel. We want to avoid this.

The daughter of Ministry of Tourism - We will offer her an upgraded room in the airport hotel, minimizing the time she needs to spend in traffic getting to the airport during morning rush hour. She will be escorted there with the complimentary hotel limousine. She will also be offered complimentary early breakfast in her room.

The business woman attending a conference in the city - We will offer an upgraded room in the hotel closest to her conference. She will be escorted there with the complimentary hotel limousine. She will also receive a voucher for 60 minutes relaxing massage.

The elderly couple - We will offer a resort 20 minutes outside the city, with quiet rooms, numerous activities for seniors and nature walks. They will be escorted there with the complimentary hotel limousine and offered a complimentary sunset cruise.

Party-loving socialite - We will offer her an upgraded suite in the hotel with the hippest club in the city. We will offer transfer by a pink Hummer limousine, similar to the one she posted on the Instagram with the tag "one day I wish...", a complimentary bottle of champagne and VIP passes to the club for her and 5 of her closest friends.

Famous travel blogger - We will give one room to him, as the purpose of his trip was visiting our hotel. His review is important and canceling or rescheduling last minute cannot be considered an option. Relocating him to another hotel would defeat the purpose of the visit.

The general manager of sister hotel - We will offer transfer to another hotel closer to the airport and an upgraded room.

The five-months pregnant woman with her daughter - we will offer an upgraded suite or connecting room in another hotel with large kids swimming pool and playground. We will offer transfer with the complimentary hotel limousine equipped with a car seat, as well as 4-hour nanny service and a 1-hour voucher for a pregnancy foot massage.

TIPS FOR THE ROLE PLAY

↳The assessor will nominate candidates to play the role of the front desk manager while she will play the role of one of the guests who is being turned down.

↳Regardless of the customer, have an opening and closing line prepared. For example, "Good morning Miss Anne! How are you today? I have some good news and some bad news. Unfortunately, our hotel has been overbooked, and we have no rooms available; however, I managed to find some options for your stay." You can always end with "You are a valuable customer for us Miss Anne, and I hope we managed to minimize your inconvenience as much as possible. I am looking forward to serving you next time."

↳Expect the customer to say "NO" as the initial reaction. When this happens, start adding to your offer. Don't offer all alternatives in one sentence. First, offer the upgraded room in a location more convenient to the customer's plan. See the reaction. Add to it the free limousine. When the client is still resistant, mention the free voucher or extra service you are offering.

↳Have a backup in mind when the customer is still not convinced. You can try offering a future free night stay at the hotel.

↳Expect the customer to add demands and be prepared to use your imagination to cater to them.
↳Keep in mind that an apparently satisfied customer doesn"t mean you passed the stage, just as much as an apparently unsatisfied customer doesn"t necessarily say that you failed the assessment.

FINAL NOTES

Handling a difficult customer will never be a black and white scenario. You are dealing with human emotions, and you can never estimate how somebody feels. Your proposed solution might work for one customer but might not work for someone else who has gone through the same experience.

Your primary focus should be on listening to the client and offering beneficial solutions to both the customer and the company. Do not go against what the company stands for to make a customer happy and of course do the best you can to solve the issue.

Once again, how you work with your group is very important, and this is what the assessors are looking for.

Work together, not against each other. This is not a competition!

IMPORTANT

↳Do not be not completely silent.
↳Do not be the center of attention.
↳Make sure that you say one or two things and then allow your colleagues to participate as well.
↳Do not be the only one talking.
↳Voice your opinion but do not try to impose it over your colleagues, even when you are sure you are right.
↳You may think that the customer is not right. That is irrelevant. Do not start debating with the team if the customer is right or wrong. The customer should always be happy with how your business handled issues.
↳Try to think from the customer's perspective.
↳If there is another candidate who is taking charge and wants to solve the issue by himself, try not to get frustrated. Just gently input your opinion once or twice then step back.
↳Be aware of your body language: smile, facial expression, posture, gestures and other non-verbal cues.
↳Smile at your team members, but only when appropriate to create a positive body language. Do not laugh when a serious matter is being discussed.
↳Do not get intimidated by the interviewers taking notes.
↳Do not glimpse at the assessors to get a clue of how you are doing.

→Do not get emotional during the role play. It is just a simulation; it does not reflect what the assessor thinks about you.
→Do not be afraid to improvise.

SIMILAR EXERCISES
- You spilled red wine on a customer's shirt. How do you deal with the situation?
- You have only 15 toys, but 25 children in the cabin. How do you handle this?
- You work in a tailor shop, and the customer's trousers are cut too short. What do you do?

2.2.6.3.2 EXERCISE 2 - ONE WORD CARDS

HIGHLIGHTS
This is an exercise in which the following capabilities are assessed:
- clear and straightforward verbal communication
- active listening
- assertiveness
- finding creative ideas and solutions
- explaining a personal point of view in a simple and concise manner
- thinking out of the box
- working as a part of the group
- accepting opinions from other team members
- agreeing and disagreeing in a constructive manner
- respecting the set timing

SCENARIO - PART ONE
Your team will receive an index card on which it is printed a profession.
Discuss with your teammates the skills a person needs to possess to carry out this profession successfully.
At the end of your debate, each team member will present a skill and the circumstances in which it will be used.
You have 10 minutes to complete the exercise.

HOW TO HANDLE THE EXERCISE
When this exercise is being used, it is usually the ice-breaker. It will be your first interaction in a small group setting, so it is important to establish a good position. You need to work harmoniously with your team members, be a good listener and think out of the box.

LANGUAGE TO USE
Guide yourself from the following examples as to the type of language to use:

When expressing an opinion
I believe we should make a list of general skills and one of the specific skills. What do you think?
When not agreeing with a team member
I can see how being organized is an attribute which will make life easier, but is it a skill without which this person wouldn't be able to perform his job?
When keeping the time
I just want to remind you that we have 5 minutes left.
SAMPLE ANSWER
Our profession was "florist." Our group has decided that the florist skills need to be divided into two categories. The first set of skills refer to the customer interaction, and we believe this to be the most important. Regardless of the talent for designing flower arrangements, a florist will need excellent skills when dealing with customers. First of all, he or she will need to be a very good listener, able to give his full attention to what the customer is saying, taking the time to understand the points being made and asking questions as appropriate. Before making a flower arrangement, he needs to understand what the customer prefers, the budget, what kind of event will it be needed for and what is the desired lifespan of the arrangement.

The florist should also be service oriented, meaning he will be actively looking for ways to help people. Buying flowers can be an emotional event, and the florist must have the subtle skill of putting people at ease.

Finally, he needs to have excellent time management skills, respecting his own time and the time of others when committing and delivering the flower arrangements.

For the second set of competencies, the florist will need to have an eye for design, color pairing, botany knowledge about cut flowers lifespan and living plants care, as well as the willingness to keep up to date and follow industry trends. This is of course needed for delivering beautifully arranged pieces.

***This sample answer above is a complete answer. This presentation should be divided among the members of the group.

SCENARIO - PART TWO
Your team will receive a second index card on which it is printed a photo of a random object.

Discuss with your teammates how this object can be used by the profession you had in the first part of the scenario. Provide at least three examples.

At the end of your debate, the assessor will nominate a team member to present your proposal.

You have 10 minutes to complete the exercise.

HOW TO HANDLE THE EXERCISE
This is the part where you need to use your imagination, thinking out of the box and be extremely resourceful with your scenario.

There is no right or wrong answer. Be open to listen to your team members, contribute at least one use of the object, even if your suggestion will not make the final presentation.
Suggest starting a list of object uses and then decide for the top 3.
SAMPLE ANSWERS
Our profession was "florist," and our object was "an apple."
First, we thought he could use the apple when building arrangements. The skin can be peeled, dried and used as decoration. The apple can be sliced, dried and as well used as decoration. The apple itself can be cut in half and used as a base for the flower arrangements. With paint, we could make stamps for the paper used to pack the arrangement. The seeds can be planted, and hopefully, an apple tree will come out of it. Also, if the apple is placed in a transparent vase with water, it can be a decorative object in the flower shop. We can cut the apple, core it and make tea-light holders. It can also be placed in a bucket of water and kids in the shop can be entertained by being given small nets to try to fish the apple out.
We can also cut it and offer it to the customers as a snack.
We also considered that the florist should eat the apple so he can have more energy to build even more beautiful arrangements, but we have dismissed this option quite quickly.
FINAL NOTES
Once again, how you work with your group is very important, and this is what the assessors are looking for.
Work together, not against each other. It is not a competition!

IMPORTANT
↦This exercise is usually used at the beginning of the assessment, to have the first glimpse into small group interaction.
↦The size of your group will be very small (3-4 people).
↦Listen before you talk.
↦Do not be entirely silent.
↦Do not be the center of attention.
↦Make sure that you say one or two things and then allow your colleagues to participate as well.
↦Do not be the only one talking.
↦Voice your opinion but do not try to impose it over your colleagues, even when you are sure you are right.
↦If there is another candidate who is taking charge and wants to run the entire show, try not to get frustrated. Just gently input your opinion once or twice then step back.
↦The sky is the limit when this exercise is being given, however always keep appropriate uses of these objects.

→Be aware of your body language: smile, facial expression, posture, gestures and other non-verbal cues.
→Smile at your team members.
→Do not get intimidated by the interviewers taking notes.
→Do not glimpse at the assessors to get a clue of how you are doing.
→Have fun!

SIMILAR EXERCISES

You will be given an individual index card showing a random object (yoghurt, pencil, toothpaste, balloon, etc.) You will be asked to find five uses for that object.

2.2.6.3.3 EXERCISE 3 - PRIORITIZATION

HIGHLIGHTS

This is an exercise in which the following capabilities are assessed:
- prioritizing
- logical thinking
- explaining personal points of view in a simple and concise manner
- working as a part of the group
- accepting opinions from the group members
- agreeing and disagreeing in a constructive manner and respecting the set timing

SCENARIO

You are a member of a space crew originally scheduled to rendezvous with a mother ship on the lighted surface of the moon. However, due to mechanical difficulties, your ship was forced to land at a spot some 200 miles from the rendezvous point. During re-entry and landing, much of the equipment aboard was damaged and, since survival depends on reaching the mother ship, the most critical items available must be chosen for the 200-mile trip. Below are listed the 15 items left intact and undamaged after landing. Your task is to rank them in order of importance for your crew. Place the number 1 by the most important item, the number 2 by the second most important, and so on through number 15 for the least important.
You have 20 minutes to complete the exercise.

Your Ranking	Item	NASA Ranking
	Box of matches	
	Food concentrate	
	50 feet of nylon rope	

	Parachute silk	
	Portable heating unit	
	Two .45 caliber pistols	
	One case of dehydrated milk	
	Two 100 lb. tanks of oxygen	
	Stellar map	
	Self-inflating life raft	
	Magnetic compass	
	20 liters of water	
	Signal flares	
	First aid kit, including injection needle	
	Solar-powered FM receiver-transmitter	

HOW TO HANDLE THE EXERCISE

There are two options to consider when starting this exercise:

Option 1

The group already has an established leader. You will be able to recognize this person because they are the ones who start talking and take charge in getting the task solved.

If this is the case, your role is to be as active as possible and volunteer for little tasks, such as keeping the time or writing the answers on the provided piece of paper.

Option 2

There is complete silence when the task is handed to you. Ask first if anybody wants to read the exercise. If nobody wants to do it or they nominate you, read the instructions to the rest of the group. Do not keep the paper to yourself, but put it in the middle of the table where everybody else can see it.

Regardless if there is already a leader or not, please keep in mind that the correct approach to a group exercise for the cabin crew position requires you, above all, to show that you are capable of working well in a team.

LANGUAGE TO USE

Guide yourself from the following examples as to the type of language to use:

When expressing an opinion
I believe we should consider first what we need to survive in that environment. What do you think?
When not agreeing with a team member
I understand what you are saying about the parachute silk being a great tool for protection; however, we should also consider that maybe the water should get a higher position. We will need it to replenish the water loss.
When keeping the time
I just want to remind you that we have 5 minutes left and ten more items to agree upon.
When making a group decision if you are the one writing the answers
So we agreed that the box of matches would be in the last position. Are we all ok with this?
ANSWERS

Your Ranking	Item	NASA Reasoning
15	Box of matches	Virtually worthless, there's no oxygen on the moon to sustain combustion
4	Food concentrate	Efficient means of supplying energy requirements
6	50 feet of nylon rope	Useful in scaling cliffs and tying injured together
8	Parachute silk	Protection from the sun's rays
13	Portable heating unit	Not needed unless on the dark side
11	Two .45 caliber pistols	Possible means of self-propulsion
12	One case of dehydrated milk	Bulkier duplication of food concentrate
1	Two 100 lb. tanks of oxygen	Most pressing survival need (weight is not a factor since gravity is one-sixth of the Earth's; each tank would weigh only about 17 lbs. on the moon)
3	Stellar map	Primary means of navigation, star patterns appear essentially identical on the moon as on Earth
9	Self-inflating life raft	CO2 bottle in military raft may be used for propulsion

14	Magnetic compass	The magnetic field on the moon is not polarized, so it's worthless for navigation
2	20 liters of water	Needed for replacement of tremendous liquid loss on the light side
10	Signal flares	Use as distress signal when the mother ship is sighted
7	First aid kit, including injection needle	Needles connected to vials of vitamins, medicines, etc. will fit special aperture in NASA space suit
5	Solar-powered FM receiver-transmitter	For communication with mother ship (but FM requires line-of-sight transmission and can only be used over short ranges)

Scoring

For each item, mark the number of points that your score differs from the NASA ranking, then add up all the points. Disregard plus or minus differences. The lower the total, the better your score.

0 - 25 excellent
26 - 32 good
33 - 45 average
46 - 55 fair
56 - 70 poor -- suggests use of Earth-bound logic
71 - 112 very poor – you're one of the casualties of the space program!
***This was published in the July 1999 issue of the NightTimes

FINAL NOTES

Unless you work for NASA and you have been trained in Moon survival skills, there is a very high chance that you and your team members will not be able to fulfill the task and give all the correct answers. That is fine and normal. How you worked together with your team and how you managed to come up with the answers are the most important aspects. This will establish if you and your team members are going to continue the Assessment Day or be sent home.

Be a good sport, encourage each other, collaborate well and learn to let go for the better of the group.

IMPORTANT

↦Take the text and highlight the critical information. It will be easier to find the important key points of the task.
↦Do not be overbearing.

↠Do not talk too much.
↠Voice your opinion but do not try to impose it over your colleagues, even when you are 100% convinced that you are right.
↠Do not be completely silent.
↠Do not raise your tone.
↠Make sure that you say one or two things and then allow other people to participate as well.
↠Stick to your task. If you are not in charge of keeping the time, do not double check with the time-keeper how much time you have available. That is their job. Trust your colleagues.
↠If there is somebody else who is overbearing and taking charge, do not get frustrated, just make sure your voice is heard at least couple of times.
↠Use an open body posture.
↠Smile at your team members, but don't overdo it.
↠Do not look at the assessors to get a clue of how you are doing.
↠The interviewers will take a lot of notes, do not get intimidated by it. This is so that they can have all the information to make a hiring decision later.

SIMILAR EXERCISES

You are part of the cabin crew when your aircraft had a technical difficulty and had an emergency landing in the jungle. You have people who are hurt, and you need to get back in the plane to take the necessary things. You are given a list of equipment that you must sort in order of importance.

2.2.6.3.4 EXERCISE 4 - TEAM BUILDING

HIGHLIGHTS

This is an exercise in which the following capabilities are assessed:
- planning and thinking ahead
- explaining a personal point of view in a straightforward and concise manner
- working as a part of the group
- respecting the boundaries of your position in a group
- accepting opinions from the group members
- agreeing and disagreeing in a constructive manner
- respecting the set timing

SCENARIO

Your goal is to build the tallest structure that you can with the materials provided.
Rules:
The structure you build must be self-standing.

You must use all the materials in the set.
You cannot use any other materials.
You can do anything you want with the materials.
Materials are:
8 sheets of paper, 3 crayons, 1 roll of tape, 10 paper clips, 1 stick glue, 10 playing cards, 3 chopsticks.
You will be judged based on the height, design, and stability of your construction.
You have 20 minutes to complete the task.

HOW TO HANDLE THE EXERCISE

This exercise requires the group to be organized and be able to build a complex structure. As not all the team members will be able to build at the same time, the best approach is that the group is divided into smaller groups, each responsible for one part of the task.

It is important that your group talks about how you will be able to achieve a tall, free-standing construction using the materials provided. You need a plan!

Once again, the group leader will take charge and suggest how to start the exercise. This is done by saying, *Should we first discuss how are we going to handle the construction before we start the work?*

The team should be divided into the following groups: the time-keeper, the planning group, the construction team and the person who will make the presentation at the end.

If you are the team leader, ask volunteers for different tasks: *Who would like to keep the time?*, *Who would like to be part of the construction team?* or *Who would like to prepare the materials?*

If you are not the group leader, volunteer for that part of the project that interests you the most and will be good at. There is no position more important than the other.

LANGUAGE TO USE

Guide yourself from the following examples as to the type of language to use:

When expressing an opinion

I believe we should start by thinking about what we can do with each material. For example, we can keep the chopsticks and crayons at the end to add height to our construction. What do you think?

When not agreeing with a team member

I see how using all the paper clips to make the base will make it sturdy, but we get a higher score if our construction has a good height. Can we find a way to save some of the paper clips to use for adding elements to make the construction higher?

When keeping the time

I want to remind you that we have 5 minutes left.

When being a part of the planning team

So we agreed that we would build a base from the glued playing cards and we will add height with rolled sheets of paper, crayons, and chopsticks. Should we hand it over to the construction team?

When being part of the construction team
The base made out of playing cards is not stable enough. We should use two crayons to stabilize it. What do you think?

FINAL NOTES

The construction you make will be a unique piece. 100 different teams will have 100 different structures, so there is no right or wrong way to build the tower.

What is vital when participating in this exercise is how you deal with your team members and what can be achieved by team effort.

Have a plan before you start building and make sure that everybody in the team has something to do. Even if you are not the team leader, if you see that somebody has been left out, just try to get them involved by asking for their opinion on a subject you raise. You will score high points with that.

How you communicate with each other is also a critical point to consider. Can you make yourself understood by the rest of the group? Do you have a good point when starting up a conversation? Are you able to let go when your opinion is not well received by the group?

The key word for this exercise is **COLLABORATION**. The task can only be achieved by joint effort. Work together!

IMPORTANT
↳Do not take over the exercise.
↳Stick to what you volunteered or what you have been assigned.
↳Voice your opinion but do not be the only one talking.
↳Do not be silent and reserved.
↳Make sure that you present your point of view, but then allow other people to debate it.
↳If there is somebody else who is taking charge and does not allow other people to participate, just make sure your voice is heard at least once.
↳Do not talk just for the sake of talking. Make sure you have a point.
↳Be realistic.
↳Smile at your team members, but don't overdo it.
↳Do not look at the assessors to read from their faces how you are doing.

SIMILAR EXERCISES
You are divided into two groups. Each group is given a bag of materials. You can exchange the materials with the other team. Your task is to build a free standing construction of at least 1 m in height.

When the group exercise is over, you will go on a break while the assessors decide which candidates will go through to the next stage of the Assessment Day.

Important points about the group exercise

↣There is no pre-established number of people to recruit. The best of the candidates will be selected. It can be all of you or none of you, depending on your performance, especially during the group exercise. Remember, this is not a competition!

↣Contribute to your group, but be mindful of your enthusiasm. You don't want to be the only one talking or doing the task all by yourself.

↣Do not sit quietly in the corner. Say at least one or two things. If you cannot contribute in any other way, at least say: *I agree with this approach* or *We are doing great!*

↣If there are misunderstandings or conflicts between members of your team, stay away from it and just focus as much as you can on completing the task with the rest of the group members.

↣The flight attendant position requires you to be able to integrate and work together with a new team every day. You need to demonstrate that you can do that during the group exercise.

↣You do not need to be in charge or just execute tasks that are given to you. You need to be contributing! Even a small idea counts.

2.2.6.4 ENGLISH TEST

Every airline has a different approach to the English test.
The exercises that follow summarize the different testing methods used by the airlines. Throughout this chapter, you can practice your grammar and vocabulary, assess your reading and understanding skills or test your creative talents when writing an essay.

2.2.6.4.1 GRAMMAR TESTS

ADVICE
- Read the entire paragraph before you look at the answer.
- Come up with the answer in your head before looking at the possible answers.
- If you are not sure, start by eliminating answers you know aren"t right.
- Read all the choices before choosing your answer.

- Don't keep on changing your answer. Usually your first choice is the right one, unless you misread the paragraph.

250 MISSING WORDS SAMPLE PRACTICE TEST

This test requires you to fill in the blanks with the correct word. You have four choices of answers. Only one is correct. As with all the other tests in this book, I recommend that you print the pages and fill in the answer. After you are done, you can correct yourself using the answer sheet at the end of this test.

1. The train station is ____ here.
A. near
B. near to
C. near from
D. nearing

2. When we woke up, everything was ____ snow.
A. covered
B. covered by
C. covered with
D. covering

3. Do earthquakes ____ often in California?
A. break
B. break out
C. happen to
D. occur

4. We had better ____ before it begins to rain.
A. leave
B. leaving
C. to leave
D. to leaving

5. A large crowd ____ in front of the court.

A. gathering
B. to gather
C. had gathered
D. had gathering

6. In winter, driving accidents occur quite _____ in the streets.
A. frequently
B. many
C. much
D. a few

7. Would you like to _____ to Mexico?
A. trip
B. voyage
C. travel
D. went

8. Most children at some stage start to have a feeling _____.
A. responsible
B. responsibility
C. of responsibility
D. to be responsible

9. Radio City Music Hall can hold _____.
A. much audience
B. a large audience
C. much audiences
D. many audiences

10. When the trees _____, there can be large forest fires.
A. become dry
B. becoming dry
C. become drying
D. drying

11.   " - What kind of work are you doing for Google?"
" - I'm _____ as a computer programmer."

A. worked
B. occupied
C. hire
D. employed

12. " - I don't want to buy anything, do you?"
" - Yes, I'd like to buy ____."
A. butter
B. much butter
C. any butter
D. some butter

13. We can ____ sports on Sunday if you'd like.
A. plays
B. has
C. does
D. play

14. ____ the hotel rooms are reserved through the summer season.
A. Almost
B. Almost of
C. Almost all of
D. Most of all

15. " - Where did you work before?"
" - I worked only minutes ____ airport."
A. from
B. from the
C. near
D. away

16. " - I don't think it will stop raining at all today, do you?"
" - No, I ____ so."
A. think not
B. not think
C. don't think
D. do think not

17. We have only another ten minutes. I think we ____.

HOW TO BECOME A FLIGHT ATTENDANT

A. hurry
B. be hurry
C. to hurry
D. should hurry

18. Many supporters showed up at the game. They were _____ the big players.
A. anxious seeing
B. anxious to see
C. to anxiously see
D. to see anxiously

19.   " - Who did you meet at the art gallery opening last night?"
" - I met many _____ people."
A. grandly
B. celebration
C. fame
D. prominent

20.   " - Dominic is not sure that the meeting will be held tomorrow."
" - But I _____."
A. certain
B. certainly
C. am certain
D. am certainly

21. My brother loves to watch football; I _____ hockey.
A. prefer to watch
B. to prefer watching
C. watch preferring
D. preferring to watch

22. Many people are waiting for the latest memo. It will _____ soon.
A. be circulate
B. circulated around
C. come near
D. come around

23. I think our family will _____.

A. be here shortly
B. shortly be here
C. here be shortly
D. here shortly be

24. Who _____ when Kevin is likely to turn up.
A. know
B. do know
C. is knowing
D. knows

25. The planning manager is _____ a new work schedule now.
A. arranging
B. arranging up
C. be arrange
D. to arranging

26.   " - Do you go out _____ during the week?"
" - Yes, we sometimes go out."
A. every often
B. in a time
C. once upon a time
D. once in a while

27. The Gordon family will move to Houston, but we hope to _____ with them.
A. keep touch
B. keep at touch
C. keep on touch
D. keep in touch

28. Maria is not very organized. How do you _____ her?
A. put up with
B. put with
C. put up to
D. putting up with

29.   " - We should buy a new TV set."
" - But our old one will do for _____."

A. a time being
B. the time being
C. a being time
D. the being time

30.   " - Do you have any idea how you will achieve the task?"
" - Yes, I have it all ____."
A. figures
B. figured for
C. figured in
D. figured out

31. My sister often ____ after breakfast.
A. goes for a walk
B. walking
C. goes a walk
D. go to walking

32.   " - Where ____ is the best place to eat pizza around here?"
" - I am sorry, I don't know."
A. are you suppose
B. do you suppose
C. supposedly
D. you suppose

33. Every person has to ____ and respect other cultures.
A. acquaint with
B. be aquatinted with
C. get acquaint with
D. getting acquainted with

34.   " - Are you ____ in trying out the new restaurant?"
" - Yes, we are."
A. cared
B. attended
C. concerned
D. interested

35. It will be hard to say goodbye to Paul and Jenny. We are ____ at the airport.

A. see them off
B. see off them
C. seeing them off
D. seeing off them

36. " - When did you get the skateboard?"
" - My father gave ____."
A. to me the skateboard last week
B. me the skateboard last night
C. to me the skateboard last night
D. last night the skateboard to me

37. When Claire got home from the cinema, ____.
A. she made a cup of tea
B. she was making a cup of tea
C. she makes a cup of tea
D. she has made a cup of tea

38. Grace believes she is the ____ young lady in the world.
A. prettiest
B. most pretty
C. most prettier
D. most prettiest

39. She managed ____ her way through the little streets.
A. to find
B. to find out
C. to found
D. to found out

40. Can you please ____ your elbows from the table?
A. move
B. move off
C. remove
D. remove off

41. I wasn't ____ with how he handled the situation.

A. please
B. pleased
C. pleasing
D. pleasant

42. " - When did Sonia and Luke arrive?"
" - They arrived here an hour ____ you did."
A. ago
B. before
C. since
D. since before

43. After ____ his homework, Amelie went out to the mall.
A. finish
B. to finish
C. finishing
D. the finish of

44. ____ go on holiday to France or Italy?
A. Do you rather
B. Will you rather
C. Would you rather
D. Won't you rather

45. " - Who was the woman I saw you talking to yesterday?"
" - She was ____."
A. the woman next door
B. the nexted door woman
C. the woman next to the door
D. the woman next by the door

46. Such rumor is always ____ to be true.
A. good
B. very good
C. so good
D. too good

47. It is important that everyone ____ his bit during the group exercise.

A. does
B. do
C. play
D. have to

48. This is the place ____ the dog was found.
A. that
B. which
C. where
D. there

49. You should buy a mobile phone. ____ you would be able to call me all the time.
A. So
B. Then
C. Well
D. Therefore

50. Thomas seems to be ____.
A. in hurry
B. in a hurry
C. on a hurry
D. hurrying

51. ____ Christmas, kids receive a lot of presents in the United States.
A. At the
B. On
C. In
D. By

52. I wish you ____ me how to make this cake last time.
A. will teach
B. would taught
C. have taught
D. had taught

53. How much money did he borrow ____ his friend?

A. to
B. of
C. off
D. from

54. " - How much bread is left?"
" - ____."
A. None
B. Nothing
C. Not some
D. Not one

55. ____ ended in 1918.
A. World War First
B. World War I
C. Firstly World War
D. World War the First

56. My sister loves music very much and has ____ of concert tracks.
A. a large collection
B. large collection
C. much collections
D. many collection

57. We couldn't enter the building. The security guard ____ let us in.
A. shall not
B. won't
C. shouldn't
D. wouldn't

58. " - Have you ever played football?"
" - Yes, I ____ played it."
A. have
B. have ever
C. have been
D. had been

59. Tina didn't go ____ this evening. She was at home.

A. somewhere
B. anywhere
C. no where
D. someplace

60. If I _____ you, I wouldn't do that.
A. am
B. was
C. were
D. had been

61. Nadine only travels to cities _____ hospitals are known to be well staffed.
A. which
B. where
C. that which
D. that

62. By my 60th birthday, I _____ married for over 31 years.
A. will be
B. will have been
C. would be
D. would have been

63. Finally, Lynn bought a _____ car.
A. red new 2012 two-door
B. 2012 red new two-door
C. new red 2012 two-door
D. new two-door red 2012

64. My mother taught me basic cooking and _____.
A. to bake
B. how to bake
C. how to baking
D. baking

65. _____ my childhood, I studied in Berlin.

A. During
B. Ever
C. When
D. While

66. Caroline's hair is blond, and her eyes ____.
A. blue
B. are blue
C. was blue
D. has been blue

67. The children ____ do their homework while listening to music yesterday.
A. was able to
B. were able to
C. would
D. could have

68. The history students ____ by the guest lecturer from England at that time.
A. were learning
B. were being taught
C. were being teaching
D. were being learned

69. " Hello! ____ Bob Harper speaking."
A. I'm
B. This is
C. There is
D. Here is

70. It is sometimes very difficult ____ in another language.
A. to make oneself understood
B. for oneself to be understanding
C. understanding oneself
D. to understand oneself

71. The soldiers rode through the city ____ of beautiful black horses.

A. over the back
B. in the back
C. back
D. on the back

72. This is the _____ spaghetti I've ever tasted.
A. more good
B. most good
C. best
D. most best

73. If Hannah asks her father, she _____ permission.
A. may have gotten
B. might have gotten
C. might get
D. maybe get

74. He fell from the roof of his house, _____ breaking his leg.
A. so
B. because
C. thus
D. whence

75. My sister lived in Vietnam for two years and my niece _____ there.
A. borned
B. born
C. was borned
D. was born

76. _____ the store manager, we don't need to come to work this Saturday.
A. According
B. According of
C. According from
D. According to

77. You _____ see the dentist if that toothache persists.

A. better
B. better have
C. have better
D. had better

78. How long does it take _____ the city center?
A. get to
B. to get
C. to get to
D. getting to

79. She loves her new job and _____.
A. works hardly
B. hard works
C. hardly work
D. works hard

80. Please fill _____ this online application form.
A. up
B. on
C. down
D. out

81.   " - I've never seen that play."
" - _____ have I."
A. So
B. Either
C. Neither
D. Too

82.   " - Haven"t you been to Houston?"
" - _____ been there."
A. Yes, I haven"t
B. Yes, I wasn't
C. No, I haven"t
D. No, I have

83.   " - Where does Steven live?"
" - He lives _____."

A. in the Perry Street
B. on Perry Street
C. at Perry Street
D. on the Perry Street

84. Is your garage _____?
A. as large as mine
B. so large as me
C. as large as me
D. so large than mine

85. I've never seen _____.
A. such a tall woman
B. so tall woman
C. such tall woman
D. as tall woman

86. Please carry this parcel _____ the next room.
A. inside
B. at
C. in
D. into

87. My sister didn't buy _____ clothes at that store.
A. one
B. some
C. a
D. any

88.   " - How often do you play golf?"
" - I play _____."
A. two times in a month
B. two times a month
C. two months a time
D. two times of a month

89. Martin started his current job _____ June 14.

A. at
B. on
C. in
D. to

90. Would you go with us if you _____ the time?
A. will have
B. have
C. would have
D. had

91. There hasn't _____.
A. been an event like this before
B. been an event like before this
C. an event been like this before
D. before an event been like this

92. You had better stay _____ home and take care of your sister.
A. at
B. in
C. inside
D. into

93.   " - Whose computer is this?"
" - It's _____."
A. the computer of my friend
B. my friend's
C. belong a friend of mine
D. one of my friends

94.   " - How do you start peeling a potato?"
" - Hold it _____."
A. on your left firmly hand
B. in your firmly left hand
C. firmly in your left hand
D. firmly on your left hand

95. It is really hard to believe _____.

A. he would do such a terrible thing
B. such a terrible thing he would do
C. to do he would such a terrible thing
D. would he do such a terrible thing

96. " - Did you fully understand what she said?"
" - ____."
A. I think so
B. So I think
C. I so think
D. So think I

97. Rachel is the woman standing ____ my sister.
A. before
B. to the front of
C. in front of
D. front of

98. ____ the audience safely left the cinema through the fire exits.
A. Every one
B. Every member
C. Every member of
D. Every all of

99. She ____ she was going to visit her sister in New York.
A. spoke that
B. talked that
C. said that
D. told that

100. We ____ our favorite singer's performance.
A. were disappointed by
B. were disappointed of
C. were disappointing
D. were disappointing in

101. I come ____ Sweden.
A. to
B. from
C. at

D. in

102. " - _____ do you go to the restaurant?"
" - Once a month."
A. How often
B. Where
C. How
D. Why

103. I like _____ on long train rides.
A. reading
B. read
C. to read
D. to reading

104. " - Ann, what to you do for a living? "
A. " - I'm a chef."
B. " - I'm fine, thanks. And you?"
C. " - I am working."
D. " - Good."

105. Alex _____ short stories when he was six.
A. can read
B. could read
C. can to read
D. can't read

106. Whose car is that?
A. It's of Kate.
B. It's Kate's.
C. It's Kate.
D. It's to Kate.

107. I _____ born in November.
A. was
B. am
C. were
D. is

108. His shop is on the second _____.

A. levels
B. ground
C. stage
D. floor

109. Where _____ Jake and Andrea at 6 pm last week?
A. are
B. were
C. was
D. have been

110. I speak Spanish and German but Mary _____.
A. don't
B. doesn"t
C. speaks
D. doesn"t speaks

111. I went to the bookstore _____ "Harry Potter."
A. for buying
B. to buy
C. to buying
D. for to buy

112. I can't find my contact lenses. Can you look for _____, please?
A. they
B. them
C. it
D. their

113. He is interested _____ learning how to speak English.
A. in
B. on
C. to
D. for

114. _____ there any food trucks on the street?
A. Are
B. Is
C. Am
D. Isn't

115. Would you like _____ for dessert, sir?
A. anytime
B. anywhere
C. nothing
D. something

116. Good evening, is Claudia _____?
A. at here
B. here
C. to here
D. for here

117. The doctor gave me a _____ for a special eye cream last year.
A. note
B. recipe
C. prescription
D. receipt

118. What _____ if the market is closed?
A. do you did
B. are you doing
C. will you do
D. did you do

119. I _____ my bike since 2009.
A. have had
B. have
C. had
D. am having

120.   " - Why are you so moody?"
" - Oh, I _____ breakfast this morning."
A. didn't have
B. don"t have
C. hadn't
D. haven"t

121. How long _____ Japanese?
A. are you learning

B. have you been learning
C. do you learn
D. you learn

122. Look! The taxi ____.
A. are coming
B. is coming
C. comes
D. come

123. We ____ the flight tickets in time.
A. don't book
B. have booked
C. haven"t booked
D. didn't book

124.   " - I have never been to Madagascar."
" - ____ have I."
A. Either
B. Neither
C. So
D. No

125. When Jack ____ back this evening, he'll do the cleanup.
A. will come
B. comes
C. come
D. shall come

126.   " - Have you visited The National Art Museum?"
" - ____."
A. Not
B. Ever
C. Already
D. Not yet

127. Would you mind ____ the window, please?
A. closing
B. to close
C. close

D. closed

128. My sister _____ the new carpet when I got home.
A. is cleaning
B. was cleaning
C. were cleaning
D. has been cleaning

129. I _____ play poker when I was 15.
A. using to
B. used to
C. wouldn't
D. couldn't

130 My aunt _____ come to our engagement party next month.
A. aren"t going to
B. isn't going to
C. isn't
D. will

131. You should _____ karate.
A. get off
B. is start up
C. take up
D. take off

132. I promise I _____ study harder for the next paper.
A. will
B. shall
C. should
D. must

133. Could you please tell me when _____?
A. does the bus leave
B. the bus leaves
C. does leave the bus
D. leaves the bus

134. Is Georgia _____ Monica?
A. tall as

B. as tall
C. taller that
D. more tall

135. _____ did you arrive?
A. How
B. When
C. Whose
D. What

136. Where is _____ library, please?
A. the nearest
B. nearer
C. the most near
D. more near

137 Look out! You _____ off the motorcycle.
A. will falling
B. are to fall
C. are falling
D. might fall

138. Is that uniform _____?
A. to you
B. you
C. yours
D. your

139. You _____ see a specialist.
A. did
B. would
C. should
D. had

140. My carry on luggage _____.
A. has been stolen
B. stolen
C. have been stolen
D. stole

HOW TO BECOME A FLIGHT ATTENDANT

141. If only I _____ smarter.
A. am
B. was
C. will
D. have been

142. Mom _____ me to go to school this morning.
A. said
B. told
C. make
D. suggested

143. I am fed up _____ this long test.
A. to do
B. to doing
C. with doing
D. for doing

144. I've spoken to a girl _____ dog got lost last week.
A. who
B. whose
C. that
D. which

145. By this time next month, I _____ all my final papers.
A. took
B. will have taken
C. have taken
D. take

146. If I were a member of the royal family, I _____ a mansion.
A. "d have
B. "ll have
C. "d had
D. have

147. They have put new speed bumps on the busy road to _____ accidents.
A. prohibit
B. prevent
C. avoid

D. forbid

148. Drive _____ otherwise you'll have your license suspended.
A. more careful
B. less carefully
C. more carefully
D. much more careful

149. You _____ to use your phone during the flight, so there's no point in leaving it on.
A. are allowed
B. have
C. aren"t allowed
D. can't

150. If they _____ next to each other on the first day of school, they wouldn't have got married.
A. hadn't sat
B. had sat
C. sat
D. didn't sit

151. It was _____ boring play that I fell asleep after 15 minutes.
A. as
B. so
C. such
D. such a

152. When I got home, someone _____ the door and windows.
A. will break
B. brokes
C. had broken
D. hadn't broken

153. She has been _____ of stealing the cat.
A. charged
B. arrested
C. blamed
D. accused

154. ____ the better team, we came in second.
A. Despite being
B. Despite of being
C. Although
D. Despite the fact

155. Don't talk to him about the educational system because he'll get ____.
A. upsetting
B. upset
C. upseted
D. up set

156. He always looks at the optimistic part and keeps his spirits ____.
A. high
B. negative
C. upset
D. angry

157. Mario hasn't worked here for a very long period of time and he is a little ____ on matters of procedure.
A. advanced
B. sure
C. on top
D. behind

158. I hope that now that they have finally read it in ____ they will understand me.
A. red and blue
B. blue and red
C. white and black
D. black and white

159. The reason why I feel so ____ today is because it's my last day of high school and nobody has sent me any congratulation presents.
A. happy
B. excited
C. serious
D. disappointed

160. She caused an impressive crisis for her company last week thus has got a ____ letter.

A. warning
B. congratulations
C. small
D. pink

161. In this tough economy, when you do your work, you cannot afford to make any kind of ____.
A. marks
B. papers
C. food
D. mistakes

162. As they rushed outside, people thought they were ____.
A. watched
B. watching
C. watch
D. have been watched

163. You should ask your sister to help you with your homework because she's ____ at physics.
A. very good
B. bad
C. normal
D. doubting

164. I know she doesn"t like your company anymore because the second you entered the room I saw her giving you a ____ look.
A. dirty
B. fine
C. happy
D. clean

165. Some people are used to only read the ____ lines in a magazine.
A. top
B. big
C. main
D. head

166. My mom told me always to check the ____ date of things I buy in the local supermarket store.

A. in
B. expiry
C. by
D. off

167. When the event finished, all the volunteers were paid ____.
A. off
B. through
C. out
D. over

168. The teacher was kind enough to ____ my wrong answer.
A. over
B. overtake
C. overdo
D. overlook

169. It is always ____ when you forget the names of your customers.
A. embarrassing
B. peculiar
C. singular
D. attitude

170. Newspapers are ____ to our university every week.
A. take
B. distributed
C. deliver
D. handling

171. In her wonderful speech, she expressed her ____ for receiving the Oscar for best actress.
A. thankfulness
B. gratitude
C. gratefulness
D. thanking

172. In ____, nothing much happened at the party, so it was a good decision not to go.
A. quick
B. briefly

C. short
D. shortly

173. At the end of the play, the audience gave the actors a standing ____.
A. ovation
B. applause
C. cheering
D. support

174. We wanted to meet at five o"clock yesterday, but Jenny didn't ____ on time.
A. give in
B. look up
C. put out
D. make it

175. I had better go back to the house; I surely don't want to ____ my welcome.
A. overstay
B. go off
C. run down
D. wear out

176. I made a big mistake by not ____ the document before signing it.
A. look through
B. called out
C. come by
D. get up

177. Steve is a wealthy person because he ____ how to earn a lot of money.
A. went through
B. checked in
C. fell behind
D. figured out

178. Lisa decided to ____ yoga as she wanted to become more flexible.
A. go against
B. take up
C. run into
D. hand in

179. I will buy this dress you since it is exactly what I have been ____.

HOW TO BECOME A FLIGHT ATTENDANT

A. calling off
B. giving away
C. taking after
D. looking for

180. Because it was going to rain, we decided to _____ the ping-pong match.
A. take out
B. put off
C. make up
D. go by

181. Before _____ for San Francisco, it is very important that I find a place to stay for my dog.
A. holding on
B. letting down
C. giving out
D. setting off

182. I am trying to _____ from my wife since I don't want her to get sick as I am.
A. take on
B. keep away
C. clear up
D. turn down

183. A lot of exotic plants species are in danger of _____ at the moment.
A. dying out
B. paying off
C. turning on
D. setting out

184. I have to _____ my paperwork once again to make sure I have covered all the important details.
A.   go over
B.   put up with
C. take after
D. pull down

185. My medical check-up results indicate that I have to _____ with my healthy choices.
A. keep on

B. let down
C. give up
D. put across

186. We haven"t been able to decide on which is the best company to _____ build our new pool.
A. fall out
B. come to
C. get by
D. look after

187. These days, there is a tendency to _____ the people who haven"t graduated high school.
A. take off
B. show off
C. turn over
D. look down on

188. The spy will be brought to trial because there are suspicions that he has _____ state secrets to the enemy.
A. backed up
B. given away
C. broken out
D. turned off

189. In order not to lose its market share, our family company must _____ the new technological developments.
A. hold up
B. drop in
C. fall apart
D. keep up with

190. It is obvious that the new law has _____ some important changes that will have a long-term effect.
A. brought about
B. broken away
C. taken in
D. come at

191. If it weren"t for the loan I got from the bank a year ago, it would have been impossible for us to _____ our coffee shop.
A. own
B. sell
C. drop off
D. take

192. Though he loved her sincerely, he respected his parent's wishes and _____ with her.
A. set out
B. turned out
C. made up
D. broke up

193. The fact that the inflation rate has _____ in recent months is not a good sign for the economy.
A. put it
B. come down with
C. given out
D. increased

194. Tablets are _____ resistant when scratched or dropped _____ phones.
A. much / than
B. so / as
C. such / that
D. far more / than

195. Ginny doesn"t have _____ much time for working _____ she would want to.
A. as / as
B. more / than
C. so / that
D. too / that

196. English is today among the three _____ native language worldwide after Chinese and Hindi.
A. the most spoken
B. the more spoken
C. much spoken
D. most spoken

197. My sleepless nights became _____ as the important deadlines approached.
A. so frequently
B. more frequent
C. as frequent
D. much more frequently

198. It is often said that the whale is an aggressive, even deadly animal, but in fact, it is not _____ many people think.
A. more vicious
B. so vicious that
C. as viciously as
D. so vicious as

199. The wardrobe was _____ big _____ it couldn't fit through the front door.
A. too / to
B. more / than
C. so / that
D. enough / to

200. The roots of the old pine near my childhood house spread out _____ nine meters in all directions and damaged the structure.
A. too much
B. as much as
C. so much
D. so many as

201. According to the recent election's results, the new party is _____ of the ten main political parties.
A. the smaller
B. smallest
C. much smaller
D. the smallest

202. Ever since the use of electric cars became widespread, Paris isn't _____ a polluted city _____ it was 20 years ago.
A. as / as
B. such / as
C. so / that
D more / than

203. The plot of the thriller was _____ it was so hard to follow.
A. more complicated
B. such complicated
C. so complicated that
D. much more complicated than

204. This apartment is so old now. ____, we like it very much and would never move.
A. Nevertheless
B. Although
C. Though
D. Despite

205. We can't ignore this crisis any longer. You have to ____ with it quickly.
A. deal
B. do
C. solve
D. beat

206. I really don't like watching soap operas. But I really do love documentaries because people are talking about their _____ lives.
A. reality
B. real
C. authentic
D. genuine

207. Has someone moved the plates ____ the table? I'm sure that plate with chocolate cake in front of Luna was mine.
A. off
B. along
C. around
D. on

208. We couldn't find the restaurant and it was getting late, ____ we took out our map.
A. so
B. and
C. but
D. if

209. Well, according to the timetable, a train should be along in _____ five minutes.
A. less
B. below
C. about
D. round

210. Martin Jones, _____ as the Gentle Bank Robber was convicted for 25 years in jail at the Central Court.
A. name
B. reputed
C. called
D. known

211. I was born about 30 km _____ Osaka but have always lived in Denmark.
A. from
B. to
C. far
D. near

212. Don't wash that blanket in hot water, _____ it will shrink.
A. unless
B. if
C. moreover
D. otherwise

213. _____ the vacation, we visited so many interesting, even magical places!
A. Along
B. Throughout
C. Moreover
D. All in all

214. It is expected that the police will charge the _____ later this evening.
A. guilty
B. suspect
C. condemned
D. arrested

215. Mrs. Whals, you should take these pills once a day. If the problem _____ more serious, immediately come back to my office.
A. goes

B. becomes
C. increases
D. develops

216. When each person has paid the entrance fee, _____ them with a picnic hamper, please.
A. provide
B. given
C. lending
D. give out

217. You are the only person in this company who ____ access to secret files.
A. has
B. takes
C. opens
D. sees

218. When we all looked at the bill, we realized that the ____ wasn't even included!
A. services
B. serving
C. serves
D. service fee

219. Kate and Mike got home to find their children ____ down the marble hallway in their socks.
A. sliding
B. skiing
C. falling
D. crashing

220. Scientists began to realize that monkeys were _____ relatives of humans.
A. remote
B. distant
C. far
D. vague

221. Six universities have accepted my application but I ____ to go to Chicago because I am in love with the city.
A. selecting
B. prefer

C. liked
D. enjoy

222. The _____ of the coastal areas from where my grandfather is from were called "Myami."
A. tenants
B. inhabitants
C. constituents
D. citizens

223. Just when you need a taxi, there isn't a single one in _____!
A. vision
B. sight
C. reach
D. existence

224. New Years Eve _____ on a Monday this year.
A. comes
B. becomes
C. falls
D. places

225. My original _____ was to reduce the budget.
A. direction
B. view
C. aim
D. destination

226. Why are you blaming your mother? You are _____ to blame for this situation!
A. strongly
B. dominantly
C. entirely
D. freely

227. You should _____ advantage of the discount as long as it lasts!
A. get
B. take
C. hold
D. have

228. She ____ working from her home.
A. stands for
B. can't stand
C. stands a chance
D. cannot

229. I don't mind ____ if you're not feeling well.
A. to drive
B. drive
C. driving
D. to be driving

230. " -Would you like to come windsurfing with us?"
" - ____ ."
A. "I'll love to."
B. "I like it."
C. "I'd love to."
D. "I'd like it."

231. "Flight number 340 from Paris to Buenos Aires is ____ now. Please proceed to Gate number 3."
A. taking off
B. bordering
C. boarding
D. departing

232. We"re thinking of taking ____ to the beach.
A. a trip
B. a travel
C. a tour
D. a journey

233. I ____ for the Boston Marathon.
A. am learning
B. am training
C. am teaching
D. am trying

234. " - Is your girlfriend better now?"
" - Oh yes, she's ____!"

A. fair
B. fine
C. kind
D. nice

235. Our plans have _____ a lot. We are moving to a different city.
A. altered
B. replaced
C. changed
D. transformed

236. They arrived ____ we were having breakfast.
A. while
B. why
C. during
D. for

237. They have adopted ____ Pug.
A. there
B. our
C. theirs
D. none

238. I'd like to ____ to the headmaster, please.
A. say
B. speak
C. discuss
D. describe

239. She never tells the truth. I don't believe _____ any longer.
A. hers
B. her
C. she
D. him

240. Fifty dollars were ____ from my bank account.
A. absent
B. present
C. missing
D. missed

241. " - What are your plans for the autumn?"
" - We _____ to South Africa."
A. will go
B. are going to go
C. will going to
D. go

242. You need to _____ one hour before the departure.
A. check through
B. find out
C. check in
D. check for

243. Molly will graduate with a degree in the _____ of agriculture.
A. aspect
B. field
C. sector
D. division

244. Lasers can measure distances with incredible _____.
A. care
B. precision
C. adjustment
D. attention

245. My two sisters were so excited, they ran downstairs and _____ immediately.
A. got ready
B. signed
C. drew
D. brought

246. This machine _____ the user's eye and registers identity.
A. regards
B. gazes
C. scans
D. views

247. The inquiry will be _____ by Kate Cosby, a former police officer.
A. overseen

B. overlook
C. overdrawn
D. overpowered

248. Though Ron's remarks seem insulting, if you see them in ____, they're innocent.
A. situation
B. context
C. relation
D. background

249. Early in the city's life, the _____ for knowledge led to the founding of the first school.
A. quest
B. pursuit
C. gathering
D. chase

250. The three mountain climbers spent two cold nights on the ____ mountain before rescuers arrived.
A. exposed
B. displayed
C. overlooked
D. revealed

ANSWERS

1	A	51	B	101	B	151	D	201	D
2	C	52	D	102	A	152	C	202	B
3	D	53	D	103	A	153	D	203	C
4	A	54	A	104	A	154	A	204	A
5	C	55	B	105	B	155	B	205	A
6	A	56	A	106	B	156	A	206	B
7	C	57	D	107	A	157	D	207	C
8	C	58	A	108	D	158	D	208	A
9	B	59	B	109	B	159	D	209	C
10	A	60	C	110	B	160	A	210	D
11	D	61	B	111	B	161	D	211	A
12	D	62	D	112	B	162	B	212	D
13	D	63	C	113	A	163	A	213	B
14	C	64	D	114	A	164	A	214	B
15	B	65	A	115	D	165	D	215	C
16	C	66	B	116	B	166	B	216	A
17	D	67	B	117	C	167	C	217	A
18	B	68	B	118	C	168	D	218	D
19	D	69	B	119	A	169	A	219	A
20	C	70	A	120	A	170	B	220	B
21	A	71	D	121	B	171	B	221	B
22	D	72	C	122	B	172	C	222	B

23	A	73	C	123	C	173	A	223	B
24	D	74	C	124	B	174	D	224	C
25	A	75	D	125	B	175	A	225	C
26	D	76	D	126	D	176	A	226	C
27	D	77	C	127	A	177	D	227	B
28	A	78	C	128	B	178	B	228	B
29	B	79	D	129	B	179	D	229	C
30	D	80	D	130	B	180	B	230	C
31	A	81	C	131	C	181	D	231	C
32	B	82	C	132	A	182	B	232	A
33	B	83	B	133	A	183	A	233	B
34	D	84	A	134	C	184	A	234	B
35	C	85	A	135	B	185	A	235	C
36	B	86	D	136	A	186	B	236	A
37	A	87	D	137	D	187	D	237	B
38	A	88	B	138	C	188	B	238	B
39	A	89	B	139	C	189	D	239	B
40	C	90	D	140	A	190	A	240	C
41	B	91	A	141	B	191	A	241	B
42	B	92	A	142	B	192	D	242	C
43	C	93	B	143	C	193	D	243	B
44	C	94	C	144	B	194	D	244	B
45	A	95	A	145	B	195	A	245	A

HOW TO BECOME A FLIGHT ATTENDANT

46	D	96	A	146	A	196	D	246	C
47	A	97	C	147	B	197	B	247	A
48	C	98	C	148	C	198	D	248	B
49	B	99	C	149	C	199	C	249	B
50	B	100	A	150	A	200	B	250	A

FILL-IN THE BLANKS SAMPLE PRACTICE TEST 1

From the list below, choose the correct word to insert in the text.

were	became	need
soul	also	creating
other	tombs	built
one	next	

The ancient Egyptians ____1____ massive public monuments for their pharaohs. But they also spent time and treasure ____2____ hidden underground mausoleums that no one was ever meant to see.

The most famed collection of such elaborate tombs—the Valley of the Kings—lies on the Nile's west bank near Luxor. During Egypt's New Kingdom the valley ____3____ a royal burial ground for pharaohs such as Tutankhamun, Seti I, and Ramses II, as well as queens, high priests, and ____4____ elites of the 18th, 19th, and 20th dynasties.

The tombs evidence elaborate preparations for the ____5____ world, in which humans ____6____ promised continuing life and pharaohs were expected to become ____7____ with the gods. Mummification was used to preserve the body so that the deceased's eternal ____8____ would be able to reanimate it in the afterlife.

The underground ____9____ were also well stocked with all the material goods a ruler might ____10____ in the next world. Treasures—like the golden masks found with King Tut—are dazzling, but the tombs ____11____ contained the more mundane.

This piece is adapted from http://science.nationalgeographic.com/science/archaeology/valley-of-the-kings/

ANSWERS
1. built
2. creating
3. became
4. other
5. next
6. were
7. one
8. soul
9. tombs
10. need
11. also

FILL-IN THE BLANKS SAMPLE PRACTICE TEST 2

From the list below, choose the correct word to insert in the text.

between	also	worth
best	who	and

The names of the communities in Cape Breton, Nova Scotia, hint at the French, aboriginal, Scottish, Irish, and English origins of the people ____1____ live here: Baddeck, Margaree, Chéticamp, Ingonish, St. Ann's. The land itself seems undisturbed through centuries, in all the rough and gorgeous glory of rock, sea, sky, and forest. Angelo Spinazzola, a kayak guide and native Nova Scotian (the product of a wave of Italian immigration in the 1900s) sees a symbiotic relationship ____2____ the people and the landscape. "There's a sort of ruggedness that feeds into the people, and a softness ____3____ gentleness in the hills."

July and August have the ____4____ weather. Both leaves and weather start turning in September and winter weather rolls in by mid-October during the Celtic Colors Festival, but the music makes it ____5____ the gamble. Explains Spinazzola, who's ____6____ a musician."People come from Scotland and Ireland to regain their roots." Golfers hit the coastal greens at the rugged Cabot Links or the more established Highland Links whenever possible.

This piece is adapted from: http://www.nationalgeographic.com/travel/canada/cape-breton-nova-scotia/

HOW TO BECOME A FLIGHT ATTENDANT

ANSWERS
1. who
2. between
3. and
4. best
5. worth
6. also

FILL-IN THE BLANKS SAMPLE PRACTICE TEST 3

From the list below, choose the correct word to insert in the text.

nose	through	forward
which	located	motion
instead	side	most

For any airplane to fly, one must lift the weight of the airplane itself, the fuel, the passengers, and the cargo. The wings generate ____1____ of the lift to hold the plane in the air. To generate lift, the airplane must be pushed ____2____ the air. The air resists the motion in the form of aerodynamic drag. Modern airliners use winglets on the tips of the wings to reduce drag. The turbine engines, ____3____ are located beneath the wings, provide the thrust to overcome drag and push the airplane ____4____ through the air. Smaller, low-speed airplanes use propellers for the propulsion system ____5____ of turbine engines.

To control and maneuver the aircraft, smaller wings are ____6____ at the tail of the plane. The tail usually has a fixed horizontal piece, called the horizontal stabilizer, and a fixed vertical piece called the vertical stabilizer. The stabilizers" job is to provide stability for the aircraft, to keep it flying straight. The vertical stabilizer keeps the ____7____ of the plane from swinging from side to ____8____, which is called yaw. The horizontal stabilizer prevents an up-and-down ____9____ of the nose, which is called pitch. (On the Wright brother's first aircraft, the horizontal stabilizer was placed in front of the wings.)

This piece is adapted from:https://www.grc.nasa.gov/www/k-12/airplane/airplane.html

ANSWERS
1. most
2. through

3. which
4. forward
5. instead
6. located
7. nose
8. side
9. motion

FILL-IN THE BLANKS SAMPLE PRACTICE TEST 4

From the list below, choose the correct word to insert in the text.

took	from	layout
have	way	other

For centuries, historians and archaeologists ____1____ puzzled over the many mysteries of Stonehenge, the prehistoric monument that ____2____ Neolithic builders an estimated 1,500 years to erect. Located in southern England, it is comprised of roughly 100 massive upright stones placed in a circular ____3____. While many modern scholars now agree that Stonehenge was once a burial ground, they have yet to determine what ____4____ purposes it served and how a civilization without modern technology—or even the wheel—produced the mighty monument. Its construction is all the more baffling because, while the sandstone slabs of its outer ring hail ____5____ local quarries, scientists have traced the bluestones that make up its inner ring all the ____6____ to the Preseli Hills in Wales, some 200 miles from where Stonehenge sits on Salisbury Plain. Today, nearly 1 million people visit Stonehenge, a UNESCO World Heritage Site since 1986, every year.

This piece is adapted from:http://www.history.com/topics/british-history/stonehenge

ANSWERS
1. have
2. took
3. layout
4. other
5. from
6. way

HOW TO BECOME A FLIGHT ATTENDANT

30-SENTENCE "FILL-IN-THE-BLANKS" SAMPLE PRACTICE TEST

Fill in the blank with the correct form of the word or words found between brackets. The correct answers are provided at the end of this test.

1. He claimed that his (bring up) _____ had caused him to become a businessman.

2. I am surprised by your (child) _____ behavior.

3. It was an easy (pregnant) _____, and she gave birth on her due date.

4. She reacted so well when she found out she had been (adopt) _____.

5. He is excluding the possibility of taking early (retire) _____ next year.

6. I am surrounded only by (teen) _____ girls. I am at the wrong party!

7. They were involved in organizing an (orphan) _____ run.

8. (adolescent) _____ is a period when parents and children need to communicate more.

9. (child) _____ is a time that is supposed to be magical.

10. He was given a blue lollipop because of his (young) _____.

11 The council told him it was (responsible) _____ to drink and drive.

12. They separated because of his (kind) _____ to the pets.

13. The keys were locked inside. (luck) _____ the kitchen window was open.

14. So many people are living in (miserable) _____ after the terrible volcano eruption.

15. Her mother accused him of being over- (ambition) _____.

16. This song shows the wonderful (sensitive) _____ of the songwriter.

17. The evening was (pleasant) _____ spent around a bonfire.

18. Due to my grandfather's (stubborn) _____ we missed the flight.

19. The thing I like about Kate is her (reliable) _____.

20. He upset her with a (tact) _____ remark about her broken arm.

21 During the last years, there was a great (improve) _____ in technology.

22. When Susan left the house, her father looked at her in (astonish) _____.

23. The clown fell on the deck, and the kids roared with (laugh) _____.

24. There was a feeling of (sad) _____ around the town.

25. Antonia has always shown a lot of (interest) _____ on tea cups.

26. Do you have (permit) _____ to borrow that dress?

27. I need an (enlarge) _____ of this x-ray scan.

28. Due to the storm, all flights had a delayed (arrive) _____.

29. Attention! The mayor has an important (announce) _____ to make.

30. They promised a (reduce) _____ in interest rates this year.

ANSWERS
1. bringing up
2. childish
3. pregnancy
4. adopted
5. retirement
6. teenagers
7. orphanage
8. adolescence
9. childhood
10. youth
11. irresponsible
12. unkindness
13. luckily
14. misery
15. ambitious
16. sensitivity

17. pleasantly
18. stubbornness
19. reliableness
20. untactful
21. improvement
22. astonishment
23. laughter
24. sadness
25. disinterest
26. permission
27. enlargement
28. arrival
29. announcement
30. reduction

40-SENTENCE REPHRASE SAMPLE PRACTICE TEST

Using the word in the brackets as a clue, rephrase the following sentences.
1. The first time Matt was here was in 2010.
(Since)
____ Matt hasn't ____.

2. It's a shame I don't have a car.
(I)
____ wish I ____ car.

3. She teaches English.
(as)
She works ____ teacher.

4. He found the soap opera very amusing.
(was)
He ____ by the soap opera.

5. I believe you should get a new hand mixer.
(I)
If ____, I'd get a hand mixer.

6. Excuse me, I can't get past you if you stay there!
(way)
Excuse me, you ____.

7. This is not my first visit to Cuba.
(time)
This is not the _____ to Cuba.

8. Nothing has been decided yet regarding the new sofa.
(no)
_____ made regarding the new sofa.

9. She returned the T-shirt to the boutique because it was too big.
(took)
As the T-shirt was too big, she _____ to the boutique.

10. If you skate faster, it's more dangerous.
(the more)
The faster _____ dangerous it is.

11. Anna started learning German six weeks ago.
(learning)
Anna _____ for six weeks.

12. Our meeting is in three weeks time.
(a)
We _____ in three weeks time.

13. Is this laptop hers?
(she)
Does _____ laptop?

14. What a pity we drank so much juice.
(only)
If _____ so much juice.

15. I prefer volleyball to handball.
(interesting)
For me, volleyball _____ handball.

16. The police officers were following the criminals.
(were)
The criminals _____ police officers.

17. Jaimie was tired, so she decided to watch an episode of her favorite TV show.
(that)
Jaimie _____ decided to watch an episode of her favorite TV show.

18. Is it necessary for me to review all the details?
(have)
Do _____ all the details?

19. How can you bear her attitude so well?
(stand)
How can you _____ her attitude?

20. Louise patted the cat's back.
(on)
Louise _____ back.

21. My mom tries really hard to help me.
(effort)
My mom really _____ to help me.

22. It's a lot easier to sell a mobile phone when it's in perfect conditions.
(much)
You can sell a mobile phone _____ when it's in perfect conditions.

23. Rebecca was too excited to read the magazine.
(that)
Rebecca was _____ she could not read the magazine.

24. You must wear a helmet when going rollerblading.
(all)
Helmets must be worn _____ going rollerblading.

25. He was told to wait on the couch by the assistant.
(who)
It was the assistant _____ to wait on the couch.

26. New York is more modern than Los Angeles.
(as)
Los Angeles is _____ New York.

27. She took a cab, but there was a traffic jam.
(have to)
She _____ a cab.

28. As the main company representative, I'd like to welcome you to our building.
(behalf)
I'd like to welcome you to our new building, _____ the company.

29. You should buy a new rice cooker.
(were)
If _____, I would buy a new rice cooker.

30. The police found out he wasn't responsible for the bank fraud.
(fault)
The bank fraud was _____.

31. "What time does the plane take off, Caroline?"
(what)
I asked Caroline _____.

32. How much does that Lamborghini cost?
(how)
I'd like to know _____.

33. Laura went to the meeting, but first she did her make-up.
(before)
_____, Laura did her make-up.

34. If he hadn't helped me, I wouldn't have passed the semester.
(without)
_____, I wouldn't have passed the semester.

35. I started this job ten days ago.
(been)
I have _____ ten days.

36. I don't want you to spend that money on a new bag.
(sooner)
I'd _____ spend that money on a new bag.

37. Your hair needs a new hairstyle.
(try)
You should _____ a new hairstyle.

38. I couldn't drink the tea because it was too sweet.
(to)
The tea _____ drink.

39. That isn't true!
(up)
You have _____!

40. I said "Well done, Mark, you have got you drivers license!"
(congratulated)
I _____ drivers license.

ANSWERS

1. Since 2010 _____ been here.
2. I _____ had a _____
3. as
4. was amused
5. I were you
6. are standing in my way
7. first time I go
8. No decision has been
9. took it back
10. you skate, the more
11. has been learning German
12. have a meeting
13. she own this
14. only we haven"t drank
15. is much more interesting than
16. were being followed by the
17. was so tired that she
18. I have to review
19. stand so well
20. patted the cat on it's
21. makes an effort
22. much easier
23. so excited that
24. all the time while
25. who said to him
26. not as modern as
27. didn't have to take

28. on behalf of
29. I were you
30. not his fault
31. what time was the plane taking off
32. how much does that Lamborghini cost?
33. Before going to the meeting
34. Without his help
35. been employed for
36. sooner not have you
37. try
38. was too sweet to
39. made it up
40. congratulated Mark on getting his

2.2.6.4.2 READING AND UNDERSTANDING TEST

ADVICE
- Practice reading English texts every day. Do not limit yourself to one topic. Become familiar with a diverse range of subjects.
- Read the entire paragraph first to understand the main idea of the text.
- Read the whole question and refer to the text to find the answer.
- When answering a question, use proper sentence building: there are the main subject and main verb, and they agree in number and tense.
- Each sentence should start with a capital letter and end with a point.

SAMPLE PRACTICE TEST 1

Read the following paragraph and answer the questions.
"Antarctica is situated over the South Pole and is divided into two separate regions called Greater Antarctica to the East and Lesser Antarctica to the West. Weather conditions when traveling to Antarctica vary greatly. In the extreme southern hemisphere, winters (June-August) are dark and spring/summer (October-February) has long hours of light. During the summers, temperatures range from around 20 degrees to as warm as 48 degrees. Due to the natural patterns of the sun however, the extended daylight hours often warm those areas that are protected from winds. Some guests find it warm enough for t-shirts and shorts! Due to the erratic weather of Antarctica, there is a very small window for traveling to Antarctica that spans from November to March. We prefer to travel during the early season which is late October through the end of November for a variety of reasons.

HOW TO BECOME A FLIGHT ATTENDANT

One of these is that even though relatively small numbers of people visit Antarctica, there are even fewer in the spring (October-November) than in the peak tourist season of December to February. Arriving in October and November is beautiful because life is emerging from a long winter's sleep and the landings are still untouched.

The trip embarks from Ushuaia, Argentina. Common air routes typically transit through Buenos Aires, Argentina or Santiago Chile."

This piece is adapted from http://www.rowadventures.com/travel-to-antarctica.htm

1. Where is Antarctica located?
2. How is Antarctica divided?
3. Is the weather the same year-round?
4. What is the temperature range during summer?
5. During what period of the year is travel to Antarctica possible?
6. Why is it better to travel from the end of October through the end of November?
7. In which city can you embark on the trip?

ANSWERS

1. 1. Where is Antarctica located?
Antarctica is located over the South Pole.
2. How is Antarctica divided?
Antarctica is divided into two separate regions called Greater Antarctica to the East and Lesser Antarctica to the West.
3. Is the weather the same year-round?
No, the weather is not the same throughout the year. Weather conditions vary greatly from summer to winter.
4. What is the temperature range during summer?
During the summer, the temperatures range from 20 to 48 degrees.
5. During what period of the year is travel to Antarctica possible?
Travel to Antarctica is possible from November to March.
6. Why is it better to travel from the end of October through the end of November?
It is better to travel from the end of October through the end of November because there are even fewer people visiting during this time. Also, the scenery is beautiful because life is emerging from a long winter's sleep.
7. In which city can you embark on the trip?
You can embark on the trip in Ushuaia, Argentina.

2SAMPLE PRACTICE TEST 2

Read the following paragraph and answer the questions.

"Hybrid tulips can be unspeakably beautiful, but they also come with a daunting array of caveats. For starters, most don't reliably return for more than two or three years—and ideal conditions are necessary for even that much longevity. Then there are the issues of disguising their dying foliage and filling the bare spots they leave behind—assuming, of course, that voles, squirrels, and other garden predators don't snatch the bulbs well before they bloom.

Growing tulips in containers, however, lets you skip most of these frustrations. In pots, tulips are eye-catching, portable, and protected. All gardeners—regardless of whether or not they've had success growing tulips inground—should give this simple technique a try.

The best time to pot up tulips is in early fall, the same as if you were planting them in the ground. Have several ready containers with outside diameters of at least 18 inches and outside heights of at least 15 inches. Using anything smaller reduces the impact of the planting and the viability of the bulbs.

If you want a certain mix of colors to emerge at the same time, choose from the same class of tulips. Short groups, such as Single Early, Double Early, and Triumph, are obvious container choices as they mix well with spring annuals and will not tower over their pot. There's no harm, however, in experimenting with taller or more exotic types, such as Parrot and Viridiflora.

Tulips of every type and color can work—just be sure to group together varieties with similar bloom times. You'll only have room for 18 to 22 bulbs per container, so successive blooming (six tulips blooming one week and another six blooming two weeks later, for example) won't look nearly as stunning as a design that flowers all at once.

To make the containers less heavy and easier to move, place an upside-down plastic grower pot at the bottom of each container. Fill the containers two-thirds full with any inexpensive, lightweight potting mix. Don't bother with fertilizer. Ignore traditional spacing guidelines, and place the tulip bulbs in a tight circular pattern. Cover the bulbs with potting mix, planting the bulbs at the same depth you would plant them in the ground: two to three times the bulb's height."

This piece is adapted from http://www.finegardening.com/how-plant-tulips-pots#ixzz4PW2StsZs

1. What is a downside of hybrid tulips?
2. What are the advantages of tulips in pots?
3. When is the best time to pot up tulips?
4. What are the types of tulips that mix well and create a beautiful color mix?
5. How many bulbs can you plant in one pot?
6. What should you ignore?
7. How deep should the bulbs be planted?

ANSWERS

1. What is a downside of hybrid tulips?

Most tulips don't reliably return for more than two or three years—and ideal conditions are necessary for even that kind of longevity.

2. What are the advantages of tulips in pots?

In pots, tulips are eye-catching, portable, and protected.

3. When is the best time to pot up tulips?

The best time to pot up tulips is in early fall, the same as if you were planting them in the ground.

4. What are the types of tulips that mix well and create a beautiful color mix?

Single Early, Double Early, and Triumph, are obvious container choices as they mix well with spring annuals.

5. How many bulbs can you plant in one pot?

You'll only have room for 18 to 22 bulbs per container.

6. What should you ignore?

You should ignore traditional spacing guidelines.

7. How deep should the bulbs be planted?

You should be planting the bulbs at the same depth you would plant them in the ground: two to three times the bulb's height.

SAMPLE PRACTICE TEST 3

Read the following paragraph and answer the questions.

"Tea, that most quintessential of English drinks is a relative latecomer to British shores. Although the custom of drinking tea dates back to the third millennium BC in China, it was not until the mid 17th century that the beverage first appeared in England.

The use of tea spread slowly from its Asian homeland, reaching Europe by way of Venice around 1560, although Portuguese trading ships may have made contact with the Chinese as early as 1515. It was the Portuguese and Dutch traders who first imported tea to Europe, with regular shipments by 1610. England was a latecomer to the tea trade, as the East India Company did not capitalize on tea's popularity until the mid-18th century.

Curiously, it was the London coffee houses that were responsible for introducing tea to England. One of the first coffee house merchants to offer tea was Thomas Garway, who owned an establishment in Exchange Alley. He sold both liquid and dry tea to the public as early as 1657. Three years later he issued a broadsheet advertising tea at six and ten pounds per pound (ouch!), touting its virtues at "making the body active and lusty," and "preserving perfect health until extreme old age."

Tea gained popularity quickly in the coffee houses, and by 1700, over 500 coffee houses sold it. This distressed the tavern owners, as tea cut their sales of ale and gin, and it was bad news for the government, who depended upon a steady stream of revenue from taxes on liquor sales. By 1750 tea had become the favored drink of Britain's lower classes.

Charles II did his bit to counter the growth of tea, with several acts forbidding its sale in private houses. This measure was designed to counter sedition, but it was so unpopular that it was impossible to enforce. A 1676 act taxed tea and required coffee house operators to apply for a license. This was just the start of government attempts to control, or at least, to profit from the popularity of tea in Britain. By the mid 18th century the duty on tea had reached an absurd 119%. This heavy taxation had the effect of creating a whole new industry - tea smuggling."

This piece is adapted from http://www.britainexpress.com/History/tea-in-britain.htm

1. How old is the custom of drinking tea?
2. When was tea brought in Venice?
3. Who imported the first tea?
4. How much did the tea cost in England?
5. What beverages suffered from tea's popularity?
6. What act was so unpopular that it could not be enforced?
7. What industry was created after the rise of the tea duty?

ANSWERS

1. How old is the custom of drinking tea?

Although the custom of drinking tea dates back to the third millennium BC in China, it was not until the mid 17th century that the beverage first appeared in England.

2. When was tea brought in Venice?

Tea reached Europe by way of Venice around 1560, although Portuguese trading ships may have made contact with the Chinese as early as 1515.

3. Who imported the first tea?

It was the Portuguese and Dutch traders who first imported tea to Europe.

4. How much did the tea cost in England?

They were advertising tea at six and ten pounds per pound.

5. What beverages suffered from tea's popularity?

Tea cut the sales of ale and gin.

6. What act was so unpopular that it could not be enforced?

Charles II did his bit to counter the growth of tea, with several acts forbidding its sale in private houses.

7. What industry was created after the rise of the tea duty?

This heavy taxation had the effect of creating a whole new industry, the tea smuggling.

SAMPLE PRACTICE TEST 4

Read the following paragraph and answer the questions.
"By the middle of the second-century bc, Rome boasted rich library resources. Initially comprised of some scattered private collections, holdings eventually expanded through the spoils of war. Even Aristotle's famed collection was among the bounty.
Julius Caesar dreamed of establishing a public library in Rome, but his vision was cut short by his assassination. After Caesar's death, Asinius Pollio acquired the necessary funds to make the dream a reality. The library was divided into two sections - one for Greek and one for Latin, serving as a model for subsequent Roman libraries. Great statues adorned the walls. Books, typically acquired through donations by authors and others, as well as through copying, were placed along the walls and readers consulted them in the middle of the room. This marked a distinct departure from the Greek model, where readers could only consult their books in an atrium away from the rest of the collection.
To serve as director of a library was a great honor. The role became a stepping stone for the ambitious government servant. Staffs consisted of slaves and freedmen, who were assigned to either the Greek or the Latin section. Pages fetched rolls from the systematically arranged and tagged bookcases and returned them. They usually transported the rolls in leather or wood buckets. Scribes made copies to be added to the collection and recopied damaged rolls while keeping the catalog up to date. Libraries were typically open during standard business hours - sunrise to midday.
Rome had only three public libraries at the time of Augustus" death in 14ad: Pollio's, one in the Porticus of Octavia, and Augustus" on the Palatine Hill. When Trajan (98-117ad) dedicated his monumental column in 112-113, a library (sectioned into the traditional Greek and Latin Chambers) was part of it. Much of the interior still exists today. The collection there grew to include some 20,000 volumes. Still, libraries remained the domain of the learned: teachers, scientists, scholars. Where were the masses to go? To the imperial baths, of course! At the baths, men and women, rich and poor could take a bath, meet with friends, play ball - and read a book. Libraries were added to the baths until the third century. A catalog of Rome's buildings from about 350ad enumerated 29 libraries in the city. But in 378, the historian Ammianus Marcellinus commented, "The libraries are closing forever, like tombs." As the Roman Empire fell, libraries seemed doomed to extinction.

This piece is adapted from http://www.history-magazine.com/libraries.html

1. In which city was Aristotle's collection kept?
2. Who made Julius Caesar's dream come true?
3. How many sections did the library have and how were they called?
4. How were the rolls transported and by whom?
5. What were the names of the libraries in Rome?
6. What did the masses prefer?
7. When were libraries added to the baths?

ANSWERS

1. In which city was Aristotle's collection kept?
Rome boasted rich library resources. Initially comprised of some scattered private collections, holdings eventually expanded through the spoils of war. Even Aristotle's famed collection was among the bounty.

2. Who made Julius Caesar's dream come true?
Asinius Pollio acquired the necessary funds to make the dream a reality.

3. How many sections did the library have and how were they called?
The library was divided into two sections - one for Greek and one for Latin.

4. How were the rolls transported and by whom?
Staff consisted of slaves and freedmen, who were assigned to either the Greek or the Latin section. They usually transported the rolls in leather or wood buckets.

5. What were the names of the libraries in Rome?
Pollio's, one in the Porticus of Octavia, and Augustus" on the Palatine Hill.

6. What did the masses prefer?
The masses prefer going the imperial baths.

7. When were libraries add to the baths?
Libraries were added to the baths until the third century.

SAMPLE PRACTICE TEST 5

Read the following paragraph and answer the questions.

"Try to imagine the world without Walt Disney. The world without his magic, whimsy, and optimism. Walt Disney transformed the entertainment industry, into what we know today. He pioneered the fields of animation, and found new ways to teach, and educate.

During his life, Walt would often try to recapture the freedom he felt when aboard those trains, by building his own miniature train set. Then building a 1/8-scale backyard railroad, the Carolwood Pacific or Lilly Bell.

HOW TO BECOME A FLIGHT ATTENDANT

The early flop of The Alice Comedies inoculated Walt against the fear of failure; he had risked it all three or four times in his life. Walt's brother, Roy O. Disney, was already in California, with an immense amount of sympathy and encouragement, and $250. Pooling their resources, they borrowed an additional $500 and set up shop in their uncle's garage. Soon, they received an order from New York for the first Alice in Cartoonland (The Alice Comedies) featurette, and the brothers expanded their production operation to the rear of a Hollywood real estate office. It was Walt's enthusiasm and faith in himself, and others, that took him straight to the top of Hollywood society.

Although, Walt wasn't the typical Hollywood mogul, instead of socializing with the "who's who" of the Hollywood entertainment industry, he would stay home and have dinner with his wife and daughters. In fact, socializing was a bit boring to Walt Disney. Usually, he would dominate a conversation, and hold listeners spellbound as he described his latest dreams or ventures. The people that were close to Walt were those who lived with him, and his ideas, or both.

On July 13, 1925, Walt married one of his first employees, Lillian Bounds, in Lewiston, Idaho. Later on, they would be blessed with two daughters, Diane and Sharon. Three years after Walt and Lilly wed, Walt created a new animated character, Mickey Mouse.

His talents were first used in a silent cartoon entitled Plane Crazy. However, before the cartoon could be released, the sound was introduced to the motion picture industry. Thus, Mickey Mouse made his screen debut in Steamboat Willie, the world's first synchronized sound cartoon, which premiered at the Colony Theater in New York on November 18, 1928.

On December 21, 1937, Snow White and the Seven Dwarfs, the first full-length animated musical feature, premiered at the Carthay Theater in Los Angeles. The film was produced at the unheard cost of $1,499,000 during the depths of the Depression. The film is still considered one of the great feats and imperishable monuments of the motion picture industry. During the next five years, Walt Disney Studios completed other full-length animated classics such as Pinocchio, Fantasia, Dumbo, and Bambi. Walt's drive to perfect the art of animation was endless. Technicolor was introduced to animation during the production of his Silly Symphonies Cartoon Features. Walt Disney held the patent for Technicolor for two years, allowing him to make the only color cartoons. In 1932, the production entitled Flowers and Trees won Walt the first of his studio's Academy Awards. In 1937, he released The Old Mill, the first short subject to utilize the multiplane camera technique.

This piece is adapted from http://www.justdisney.com/walt_disney/biography/long_bio.html

1. How did Walt Disney transform the entertainment industry?
2. Where did he and his brother set up their store?

3. What was the secret of his popularity in Hollywood?
4. How was he socializing?
5. When did Walt Disney create Mickey Mouse?
6. What is Steamboat Willie?
7. How much did it cost to make Snow White and the Seven Dwarfs?
8. What were other animated classics created afterward?
9. What allowed Walt Disney to make colored cartoons?
10. When did he win his first Academy Awards?

ANSWERS

1. How did Walt Disney transform the entertainment industry?

Walt Disney transformed the entertainment industry, into what we know today. He pioneered the fields of animation, and found new ways to teach, and educate.

2. Where did he and his brother set up their store?

Pooling their resources, they borrowed an additional $500 and set up shop in their uncle's garage.

3. What was the secret of his popularity in Hollywood?

It was Walt's enthusiasm and faith in himself, and others, that took him straight to the top of Hollywood society.

4. How was he socializing?

In fact, socializing was a bit boring to Walt Disney. Usually, he would dominate a conversation, and hold listeners spellbound as he described his latest dreams or ventures.

5. When did Walt Disney create Mickey Mouse?

Three years after Walt and Lilly wed, Walt created a new animated character, Mickey Mouse.

6. What is Steamboat Willie?

Mickey Mouse made his screen debut in Steamboat Willie, the world's first synchronized sound cartoon, which premiered at the Colony Theater in New York on November 18, 1928.

7. How much did it cost to make Snow White and the Seven Dwarfs?

The film was produced at the unheard cost of $1,499,000 during the depths of the Depression.

8. What were other animated classics created afterward?

During the next five years, Walt Disney Studios completed other full-length animated classics such as Pinocchio, Fantasia, Dumbo, and Bambi.

9. What allowed Walt Disney to make colored cartoons?

Walt Disney held the patent for Technicolor for two years, allowing him to make the only color cartoons.

10. When did he win his first Academy Awards?

In 1932, the production entitled Flowers and Trees won Walt Disney the first of his studio's Academy Awards.

2.2.6.4.3 ESSAY WRITING

ADVICE

- Read the topic carefully and make sure you understand it.
- Always decide on what you are going to write before you start. Make a list of your main points.
- It should be easy to identify the introduction, development, and conclusion. Each section should have at least one separate paragraph.
- Write in a clear and large script.
- Address the entire question or statement, not just part of it.
- By the rules of English punctuation, each sentence should start with a capital letter and end with a point, question mark or exclamation point.
- Write short, simple, complete sentences. This style sounds strong in English.
- Make sure that each sentence has a clearly identifiable main subject and main verb and that they agree in number and tense.
- Use a variety of sentence structures: question, passive voice sentence, conditional sentence, complex sentence, etc.
- Use specific examples or reasons to support your ideas.
- Stories or examples from your personal life are best.
- Remember, no one is checking up to see if these stories are true.

SAMPLE PRACTICE ESSAY

If you could rule any country in the world, which country would that be and what would you do?

EXAMPLE ANSWER

If I were given a chance to run any country in the world, I would choose Nepal. I visited this country five years ago, and I was amazed by the hospitality and the simple and humble happiness that can be seen in Nepali people.

The country has some of the most amazing scenery in the world, with numerous protected UNESCO World Heritage Sites, fantastic mountain trails, and untouched nature.

In the same time, though, a big part of Nepal's population lives in extreme poverty, and I would like to focus on making their life better.

I believe that the only way to help people living in poverty is through education. Most people in the countryside stop sending their children to school because they need help around their house. I would encourage people sending their kids to school by offering a small allowance to help the family to work their fields or keeping their animals while the children are learning.

I would also introduce a broader range of practical courses such as basics of building a small business, manufacturing, tailoring, artisanal work, restaurant management, tourist guide course, English, and bookkeeping.

On a larger scale, I would focus on tourism and expand the range of services that are available for the tourists visiting the country. For the time being, most people coming to Nepal are mountain enthusiasts who are passionate about trekking and nature. Nepal has so much more to offer. I would start a series of short TV documentaries and 30-seconds commercials with highlights of Nepal's culture and possibilities. These will be broadcast on international networks such as Discovery Channel, National Geographic, CNN and other TV channels with broad international coverage.

The documentaries will be focusing on architecture - the buildings and temples from the 15th century that still exist today, ancient cities, Tibetan monks refugee camps, yoga and relaxation retreats, as well as Nepali art classes and workshops.

Of course, all of this would be just the beginning. I believe it takes continuous and sustained effort to achieve a better standard of living, from both the government authorities and the people.

SAMPLE PRACTICE ESSAY TOPICS

1. Name three things that you like and three things you don't like about yourself and why?
2. What is your biggest regret?
3. Describe your last vacation.
4. Describe what would you do if you had the opportunity to travel the world.
5. In your opinion, what is the most important aspect (for example, altruism, intelligence etc) that a person should have to be successful in life?
6. Describe what would you do if two persons from different cultures had an argument.
7. If you had to recommend a place to visit in your country what would it be and why?

8. List two customs from your country that you would like other people to learn about.
9. Present the most common dishes of your country or city.
10. What is your favorite movie character and why?

Important points about your English Test

↠Like with any other language, the key to mastering it is practice. Read whatever you can get your hands on, write whenever you have the opportunity (then run a spell check through your work) and talk to whoever will listen.

↠Study the basics of the language and move within safe territory. Mastering present tense, past tense and future tense is all you need for a good start. Don't take the hard way and use complex terminology or sentences unless you master them.

↠Improve your vocabulary by reading online and use a dictionary for the terms that are not familiar to you.

↠Take your time during the test to read and understand the instructions fully.

2.2.6.5 MATH TEST

The math test is not common to all airlines. Some of them like to give the candidate this test, while some other prefer to not do it. Math sounds scary, but don't think that you need to have advanced knowledge to pass this test. Basic logic and 8th grade math skills is all you need. The reason for this test is for the airline to see that you will be able to successfully sell duty free items, count the stocks and keep the correct time.

SAMPLE PRACTICE MATH TEST

Do the following calculations without using a calculator. The correct answers are provided at the end of the test.

1. It is 02:00 in London. Dubai is 3 hours ahead of London. What time is in Dubai?
A. 05:00
B. 11:00
C. 07:00
D. 01:00

2. A perfume costs 80 USD. The passenger wants to pay in his local currency, the United Arab Emirates Dirham AED. The conversion rate is 1 USD=3,64 AED. How much does the passenger need to pay for the perfume?
A. 20 AED
B. 21,9 AED
C. 291,2 AED
D. 1286 AED

3. Your flight departs at 08:20 and arrives at 13:50. What is the flying time?
A. 5:30
B. 6:15
C. 2:10
D. 4:30

4. During the flight you have sold the following items from the duty free: 2 cartons cigarettes - $10 each, 3 perfumes - $47 each, 1 ladies watch - $84, 1 gents watch - $110 What is the total amount you sold during the flight?
A. $251
B. $147
C. $355
D. $1398

5. Do the following calculations:
A. 12 + 398 + 27 + 1987=
B. 50 - 10,98=
C. 10,58 - 5.36 =
D. 2,78 + 3,99 + 14,50=

6. A guest wants to buy 2 perfumes and 1 carton of cigarettes. 2 perfumes=$30,48 each, 1 carton cigarettes=$10. He gives you $100. How much money do you need to give him back?
A. $40,48
B. $45,96
C. $29,04
D. $70,96

7. Convert $1500 in the following currencies:
AED knowing that 1 USD (1$)=3,68 AED
EURO knowing that 1 USD (1$)=0,78 EUR
GBP knowing that 1 USD (1$)=0,63 GBP

HOW TO BECOME A FLIGHT ATTENDANT

8. Your flight duty started at 11:00 and lasted 7:20. At what time did you finish your duty?
A. 17:20
B. 18:20
C. 07:20
D. 18:00

9. What is 10% of $95?
A. $15
B. $9,50
C. $950
D. $10

10. It is 10:20 in London. New York is 5 hours behind. What time is in New York?
A. 15:20
B. 10:15
C. 05:20
D. 07:20

11. How much is 159 x 59?
A. 9381
B. 10258
C. 598
D. 1547

12. A guest wants to buy 2 make-up items and 1 perfume. 1 perfume costs $30,48 and 1 make-up item costs $125. He gives you $400, then asks for one carton of cigarettes that costs $20. How much money do you need to give him back after the added carton of cigarettes?
A. $99,52
B. $45,36
C. $120,58
D. $70,58

13. What is 20% of $154 divided by 4?
A. $32,56
B. $7,7
C. $56,96
D. $10,23

14. Your flight departs at 03:40 and arrives at 14:35. What is the flying time?
A. 10:55
B. 8:25
C. 8:15
D. 13:30

15. Your flight duty lasted 6:50 hours. You started at 12:00. At what time did you finish your duty?
A. 17:50
B. 18:50
C. 05:30
D. 06:50

16. A toy costs 150 USD. The passenger wants to pay in his local currency, the Canadian Dollar CAD. The conversion rate is 1 USD=1.3085 CAD. How much does the passenger need to pay for 2 toys?
A. 300 CAD
B. 392,55 CAD
C. 569,3 CAD
D. 452 CAD

17. It is 15:00 in Las Vegas. Brussels is 9 hours ahead of Las Vegas. What time is in Brussels?
A. 00:00
B. 11:00
C. 23:00
D. 06:00

18. Do the following calculations:
A. 154 + 356,35 + 295 + 1779=
B. 60,38 -12,76=
C. 10,43 - 8.69 =
D. 2,23 + 1,99 + 20,50=

19. A guest wants to buy 5 bottles of champagne. 1 bottle of champagne costs $130,56. He gives you $600. Then he changes his mind and ask for 3 bottles of champagne and one bottle of wine. 1 bottle of wine costs $123,25. How much money do you need to give him back after he changes his mind?
A. $110

B. $120
C. $85,07
D. $45,69

20. Your flight departs at 5:40 and has a flying time of 3 hours and 50 minutes. At what time to you arrive?
A. 9:30
B. 9:25
C. 10:15
D. 12:30

21. 3 bracelets cost 540 USD. The passenger wants to pay in his local currency, the English Pound (GBP). The conversion rate is 1 USD=0.8025 GBP. How much does the passenger need to pay for one bracelet?
A. 152,96 GBP
B. 22 GBP
C. 200 GBP
D. 144.45 GBP

22. Do the following calculations:
A. 248,69+458,325+300=
B. 1238,96-458.45=
C. 478.36 x 7 =
D. 458 x 4 + 3,25=

23. It is 08:56 in Madrid. Istanbul is 4 hours ahead of Madrid. What time is in Istanbul?
A. 05:56
B. 12:56
C. 04:26
D. 09:06

24. What is 65.36% of $500 multiplied by 3?
A. $578,36
B. $100,58
C. $980,4
D. $984,4

25. How much is 358,369 + 457,698?
A. 695,36

B. 816,067
C. 789,5
D. 4567,69

ANSWERS
1. A
2. C
3. A
4. C
5. A. 2424 —— B. 39,02 —— C. 32,94 —— D. 21,27
6. C
7. $1500 = AED 5520 = EUR 1170 = GBP 945
8. B
9. B
10. C
11. A
12. A
13. B
14. A
15. B
16. B
17. A
18. A. 2584,35 —— B. 47,62 —— C. 1,74 —— D. 24,72
19. C
20. A
21. D
22. A. 1007,015 —— B. 780,51 —— C. 3348,52 —— D. 1835,25
23. B
24. C
25. B

2.2.6.6 PSYCHOMETRIC TEST

One of the tests mostly used in interviewing for the cabin crew position is the 16PF or the Sixteen Personality Factor Questionnaire. This is a multiple-choice personality questionnaire, and it measures the following factors:
Warmth - Reserved vs. Warm
Reasoning - Concrete vs. Abstract
Emotional stability - Reactive vs. Emotionally stable
Dominance - Cooperative vs. Dominant
Liveliness - Serious vs. Lively
Rule-consciousness - Expedient vs. Rule-conscious
Social boldness - Shy vs. Socially bold
Sensitivity - Objective vs. Sensitive
Vigilance - Trusting vs. Suspicious
Abstractedness - Practical vs. Imaginative
Privateness - Forthright vs. Private
Apprehension - Self-Assured vs. Apprehensive
Openness to change - Traditional vs. Open to change
Self-reliance - Group-oriented vs. Self-reliant
Perfectionism - Tolerates disorder vs. Perfectionistic
Tension - Relaxed vs. Tense

This is not a pass or fail stage on the assessment day, but more of a tool to show the employer what is your personality.
You will be asked to take this test online or on paper and will be given 40-50min to complete it. There are many questions (sometimes as many as 189), and a lot of them will be repeating and rephrasing, so just tell the truth.

2.2.6.7 RAVEN TEST (IQ TEST)

Some candidates - but not all, are also asked to take the Raven test. This is a non-verbal multiple choice test that measures general intelligence. You will be given an image and asked to identify the missing element that completes a pattern.
The test includes 60 questions. You have 40 minutes to complete the test.
This is how a sample looks like. You must choose from the six patterns the one that matches the sample image.

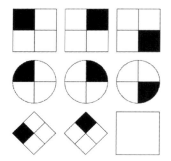

The correct answer is 4.

Important points about the Assessment Day

→ Get at the location at least 30 minutes earlier.
→ It's going to be a very long day, so as much as you can, rest well the night before.
→ Prepare your documents in advance.
→ Bring with you water, money for a coffee and something you could eat for lunch.
→ The location of the assessment day is probably a 4* or 5* hotel. The price of coffee or lunch there is quite high. Make sure you have sufficient money with you.
→ Bring a pen and a writing pad.
→ If you travel from another city, bear in mind that if you pass through all the stages of the Assessment Day, you will be invited for the final interview which sometimes takes place the next day. Plan for transportation and accommodation accordingly.
→ Exchange phone numbers and email addresses with the people who made it with you until the last stage.
→ SMILE and be friendly with EVERYBODY.

2.2.7. FINAL INTERVIEW

After the assessment day, the successful candidates will be invited for a final interview.
This will be a 1-on-1 conversation with one of the assessors or sometimes a 2-on-1 with both assessors. At this point, the interviewer will ask you a series of questions to establish your drive and motivation, as well as examples of situations you previously handled. The types of questions vary from open-ended questions such as "Tell me about yourself" to yes or no questions such as "Have you ever had a deadline?". There will be questions from your CV - "Tell me about your last job" and

questions to find out more about your personality and work style "Do you prefer to work in a group or alone?"

This is finally your chance to say and show everything that was not obvious yet.

Remember! You made it so far! They are almost convinced that you are the perfect person for the job. This is your last chance to shine and prove them how good you are and what a great addition you will be to their team!

2.2.7.1 MAKING A GOOD IMPRESSION DURING THE INTERVIEW

Being nervous is okay. It would be a bit unnatural to not be nervous at this point.

Your voice might be trembling; your hands might feel shaky or sweaty, even your knees might get a bit wobbly.

Don't worry about the interviewer seeing your nervousness. It shows that you care about the result of the interview and getting the job is important to you.

Once you start talking to them, you will forget all about it.

The recruiters are professionals, and they will do all they can to make you feel relaxed and give your best.

Here is some advice on how to behave during the 1-on-1 conversation.

DO

✓Maintain eye contact and smile.

✓If you are seating at a table, put your hands together and place them on the table. If you are seating on a chair, put your hands together and rest them on your lap.

✓Keep your legs straight or cross your ankles.

✓Talk clearly. Use simple words to describe the situation.

✓Answer the question.

✓Always present your skills or qualities.

✓Ask questions at the end if given the opportunity.

DO NOT

✖Bite your nails.

✖Look down at your shoes.

✖Put the elbows on the table.

✖Sit cross-legged or with your legs too parted.

✖Blabber if you are not sure of the answer.

✖Talk bad about your current or past employer or colleagues.

✖Complain.

✖Say, "I don't know."

✖Make jokes.

2.2.7.2 101 QUESTION AND ANSWERS FOR THE FINAL INTERVIEW

This chapter includes 101 Questions and Answers for the cabin crew final interview. Do not learn the answers that I am giving you by heart. Take the time and come up with your own answers that apply to your experience and background.

The best way to approach this is by printing the next pages, fill in your answer in the space provided and go through them before your interview. This way you will not be surprised when a question comes up.

1. Tell me about yourself.

- Remember to stay professional during your final interview. This question is meant to ask you about your career and detailed work history. It is not about your childhood, home or hobbies.
- You interviewing for a cabin crew job, so your response should be focused on the relevant customer service job experience.
- Try to keep it short; this question is just a conversation starter.
- Do not reveal information that you don't want your future employer to know.

SAMPLE ANSWER

"I have been working for the past four years for Company A. I started out as a part-time junior sales associate and have been promoted to a senior sales associate, and most recently to store assistant manager. Meanwhile, I graduated from College B with a major in Economic Studies."

YOUR ANSWER

2. Why do you want to work for our airline?

- Do not go to your interview without doing some research about the company you would like to work for. Browse their website and read the "About us" or "History" sections.
- If you participate in an Open Day, most of the time the first part of the day will consist of a series of informative videos about the airline, how it was created, plans of expansion, financial results, life in their city, career prospects and other relevant information. Use the information you learned to answer this question during the final interview.
- Do not explore unknown territory. If the interviewer brings up a certain subject that you don't know much about, be honest and tell them so.

SAMPLE ANSWER

"I know that your company has been one of the fastest growing airlines in the world, with numerous awards won (give some examples here) and openness towards cultural diversity. I would be honored to be part of such an enthusiastic team and contribute with my excellent customer service skills."

YOUR ANSWER

3. Do you know anyone who works for us?

- Only answer yes if it is someone you want the company speaking with. However, you may have to answer yes if it is a family member.
- Do not discuss people you know who you do not like or cannot count on for an outstanding personal reference.
- Do not bring up cabin crew you follow on social media.
- Be extremely selective when answering this question in a job interview, but don't lie if the interviewer asks you about a particular employee working for the airline.

SAMPLE ANSWER

"Yes, I know Mary Smith, she has been a cabin crew for your airline for the past five years."

YOUR ANSWER

4. Why do you want to be a Flight Attendant?

- This answer should be very personal. The more details you give, the better.
- Tell the story of the first time you encounter a flight attendant or the first time you traveled on a plane.
- List a couple of features about the flight attendant job that you admire, and you want to pursue.

SAMPLE ANSWER

"The first time my parents took me on a plane I was seven years old. We were going to Greece on summer holiday. It was then I saw the prettiest woman. She was tall and had beautiful brown hair and red lipstick. She gave us toys and talked to us like we were grownups. I remember that whenever we were in restaurants, the waiters would ask our parents what we want to eat; but not her. She asked us, the kids if we like to eat chicken and then she gave us the food. In the end, she even brought a small note from the pilot congratulating us for our first flight. This memory sticks with me after all these years. I want to be a flight attendant because I wish I can leave such a powerful memory in somebody's life."

YOUR ANSWER

5. What makes a good cabin crew?

- List couple of skills that makes not only a good cabin crew but also a good employee.
- Only talk about personality traits that you have and would be able to show to your interviewer.
- Stay away from the non-inspired answer: "a caring person with a warm smile."

SAMPLE ANSWER

"I believe that a good cabin crew is somebody who enjoys meeting new people, a good listener and someone who is capable of treating people as individuals and make them feel special."

YOUR ANSWER

6. What can you do for us that someone else can't?

- This is the time where you have to be comfortable in praising yourself.
- Talk about your record of getting things done and mention specifics from your resume or list of career accomplishments.
- Say that your skills and interests, combined with a history of getting results, make you valuable.
- Mention your ability to set priorities, identify problems, and use your experience and energy to solve them.

SAMPLE ANSWER

"My skills in dealing with customers and my interest for outstanding service and excellent job performance will make me a valuable employee for your airline."

YOUR ANSWER

7. What do you find most attractive about this position? What seems least attractive about it?

- List three or four attractive factors of the job.
- Make sure that the attractive elements are not listing only the benefits you get as a cabin crew, such as "free travel, 5-star hotels, etc."
- Mention a single, minor, unattractive item.

SAMPLE ANSWER

"I am very excited to have the chance to meet so many people from so many different cultures. I also think that the opportunity to see the world and the flexible schedule is a very attractive part.

On the other hand, as this is the first time for me to consider relocating, I am sure I will miss my family back home."

YOUR ANSWER

8. What is your definition of the cabin crew position?

- Keep your answer task oriented.
- Research the airline's careers website and see the description they give to the role.
- Think regarding responsibilities and accountability.
- Make sure you understand what the position involves before attempting an answer.

SAMPLE ANSWER

"The cabin crew primary responsibility is the safety and security of the passengers as well as making sure the aviation regulations are followed. Also, ensuring all guests have a pleasant experience with the airline and that they will return their business to us. When necessary, make sure all complaints are addressed and solved in an efficient manner.

To put it in fewer words, I believe the cabin crew is the airline's ambassador in delivering service excellence."

YOUR ANSWER

9. What do you ultimately want to become?

- This could be a trick question.
- Your reply should be referring to your professional life only.
- You are interviewing for a cabin crew position in the Middle East, so do not talk about how you want to become a scuba diving instructor in the Great Barrier Reef.
- Don't talk about becoming an executive in the company or perhaps applying for the interviewer's job.

SAMPLE ANSWER

"I want to become a successful and reliable employee for the airline. Eventually, I would like my career to progress towards the in-flight purser position."

YOUR ANSWER

10. What values will you bring to this company?

- List at least three of your personality traits that will benefit the airline.
- Be very specific.
- Do not start explaining how each of your values might benefit the company.

SAMPLE ANSWER

"I can contribute with my great attention to details, a track record of excellent customer service and my ambition to be the best in the job I do."

YOUR ANSWER

11. At what point in life did you choose this profession?

- Talk about the people who influenced you to choose your professional path.
- Don't say you chose your major in college because you failed out of your first choice and this one seemed easy enough.
- Don't say you ended up having this job because nobody else would hire you.
- The interviewer wants to know you will be passionate about the work you plan to perform for them.

SAMPLE ANSWER

"I always knew that my career would be working with and for people. When I was in high school, I had a summer job where I had to do the quality check at a plastic gloves factory line. While I was grateful to have the opportunity to learn and make some money, there was no interaction with others, and it was then I realized this type of work was not for me. On the other hand, I was at my highest performance and happiness on the job when I was surrounded by customers and provided them with care and solutions. My "Communications" teacher in high school was my mentor and inspired me to choose my major. Working with customers every day, meeting and interacting with new people from various cultures and backgrounds would be my dream career."

YOUR ANSWER

12. Tell me about your dream job.

- Stay away from a specific position.
- If you say another job, you will give an impression that you might be dissatisfied with the cabin crew job. If you say cabin crew, then your credibility might be questioned.
- Talk about the positive aspects that the job will bring to your life, rather than name a job title.

SAMPLE ANSWER

"My dream job will give me the opportunity to travel and discover new cultures and interesting people. It is the work that gets me excited to wake up every day, be challenged to think outside of the box and continually learn."

YOUR ANSWER

13. Why do you think you would do well at this job?

- Talk about how you progressed towards becoming the valuable employee you are today.
- Keep your answers short, but provide adequate information to respond to the question.
- The job interview is not the time to discuss the philosophical implications or moral dilemmas you pondered when selecting your career.

SAMPLE ANSWER

"I have five years customer service experience. During this period I learned how to manage various situations to achieve customer satisfaction. I learned to be flexible and always consider the point of view of the people around me. I believe that I can apply all my knowledge and experience while working as a flight attendant, as I think that the aviation environment requires the highest customer satisfaction, as well as innovative problem-solving skills."

YOUR ANSWER

14. Why are you leaving your present job?

- Be brief, to the point, and as honest as you can without hurting yourself.
- If you were laid off in a mass jobs cutback in your company, say so. Otherwise, indicate that the move was your decision - the result of your action.
- Do not mention any conflicts.
- Remember that your references are checked, so be honest.

SAMPLE ANSWER

"I want to have the experience of relocating to another country and explore new cultures. I believe that I have achieved my full potential in my current company. I am looking forward to making the next step and work for one the biggest airlines in the world."

YOUR ANSWER

15. What are the responsibilities of your current/last position?

- The description of the responsibilities should match what is written in your CV.
- This is the time when you can expand and explain more than the three bullets you included in your resume.
- Be specific.

SAMPLE ANSWER

"I work as a customer service assistant in a 5-star hotel. I am responsible for the well-being of the hotel's guests from the moment they arrive on the property until their departure. I ensure the welcome packages are in order before the estimated arrival time of our guests, I follow up the issues that might arise during check-in as well as the last minute requests and arrange special tours or parts of the vacation package. During their stay, I follow up that their experience is excellent and address the issues that are brought to my attention. Before departure, I make sure that the payments are correct and all charges are communicated to the guests, as well as arrange the airport transfer."

YOUR ANSWER

16. In your current/last position, what features do you like the most? The least?

- Be positive. Describe more features that you like than disliked.
- Don't bring up personal problems.
- If you make your last job sound terrible, an interviewer may wonder why you remained there until now.

SAMPLE ANSWER

"I enjoy the daily interaction with my customers. I like that there are no two days the same and I am challenged every day to find new ways to achieve customer satisfaction. I also like my team, and my supervisor has been a real inspiration. I have learned a lot doing this work.

I wish though that I had more time off so I could further pursue my education with a distance learning online course."

YOUR ANSWER

17. What have you learned from the mistakes you made on the job?
- Do not say that you never made a mistake on the job.
- Everybody makes errors, and it is brave to admit to them.
- Make it a small, well-intentioned mistake and mention the positive lesson you learned from it.

SAMPLE ANSWER

"I learned that everybody makes mistakes. However, the most important thing is to acknowledge when that happens and ask myself what have I done and what could I do differently next time so that the outcome will be positive."

YOUR ANSWER

18. How successful have you been so far?
- Present a positive and confident picture of yourself, but don't overstate your case.
- Say that, all-in-all, you're happy with the way your career has progressed so far.
- The most convincing confidence is the quiet confidence.

SAMPLE ANSWER

"I feel that I have done quite well both in my career and my education. I studied a major I was passionate about and my career in customer service satisfies and motivates me to learn new things continuously."

YOUR ANSWER

19. What have you been doing since your last job?

- This question is asked if there is an employment gap in your CV.
- Focus on specific activities, and highlight what is keeping you busy and organized. Make sure these activities emphasize self-improvement such as staying healthy or furthering your education.
- Do not answer the question with "nothing" or appear indecisive.
- During a job interview, the recruiter wants to find out more about your personality. Are you ambitious? Do you work hard? Are you motivated? These are the kind of workers they want to hire, so try and give an answer that highlights these qualities.

SAMPLE ANSWER

"I have been focusing on broadening my knowledge about online marketing. I have been reading many books and studies on the subject as I am planning to take a distance learning course. Also, I started running, and my goal is to complete a half marathon by the end of the year."

YOUR ANSWER

20. What have you done in the past year?

- This is the time to discuss the educational opportunities that you had in the past year.
- Discuss that education (including self-education) is a lifelong process for you.
- Make sure the interviewer understands that you are somebody who is constantly trying to improve and contribute to the well-being and success of the company.

SAMPLE ANSWER

"As I was recently promoted to the role of supervisor over a team of 5 people, I participated in my company's e-learning program and took three courses on performance management. I am trying to read as much as possible on the subject to improve my knowledge and also help my colleagues perform better."

YOUR ANSWER

21. Where would you like to be in your career five years from now?

- Refer to a career path with the airline.
- Show that you are an ambitious person, but keep your answers realistic.
- Do not say that your career plans do not stretch for such a long time and you only want to get married and be a stay-at-home mom or dad.

SAMPLE ANSWER

"In 5 years I wish I had gained a vast experience in this field, broaden my service delivery and aviation knowledge. My dream is to become a purser on the Airbus 380."

YOUR ANSWER

22. Are you willing to put the interests of the organization ahead of your own?

- Do not worry about the deep ethical and philosophical implications at this point.
- This is a loyalty and dedication question.
- If you're not sure of what they mean, ask for a specific example.
    SAMPLE ANSWER
"Yes!"
    YOUR ANSWER

23. What are the positive traits you don't have?

- This can be a trick question.
- Answer honestly, but don't go into details. Keep your answers short and professional.
- Focus on traits you can receive education for, but don't currently have. Don't reveal any information you want to keep from the interviewer.
- Avoid character traits like honesty, hardworking, reliability, and dedication as these are qualities you want the interviewer to believe you possess during a job interview.

SAMPLE ANSWER

"I know that diversity is very important in a multicultural company such as yours. My mother tongue is English, and I wish I spoke a second language to contribute with and give me a deeper understanding of the people I will encounter."

YOUR ANSWER

24. What skills or qualities you think are important for dealing effectively with customers?

- Provide an example of when you have displayed these.
- Refer to what you consider to be the most important qualities that are also relevant to the cabin crew job.
- List 2 or 3 skills in the customer service field that you can give examples for.

SAMPLE ANSWER

"I believe it is crucial to have active listening skills, be empathic, knowledgeable and one step ahead. It's better to prevent something than to cure it. I once had a group of 30 people coming into the restaurant for dinner. I knew that when dealing with such large groups, I will have to be very organized with my team and have good coordination with the kitchen. I asked them before the start of the service if they wanted to pay as a group or separately, so we could organize their bills in advance. I also managed to communicate with the kitchen so that everybody got their appetizers and main courses in the same time and they could enjoy their meals together. Drinks were also served efficiently. I achieved this by delegating specific tasks to different waiters. Some were responsible for bringing the food; one was responsible for replenishing the drinks, while I oversaw that the group was satisfied with the service and any extra requests were attended to in a quick and efficient manner. At the end of the night, the group leader said that by far this was the best experience they had in a restaurant since the beginning of their tour. This gave my team and me the great motivation that we were doing a good job."

YOUR ANSWER

25. Do you work better in a team or alone?

- This is not an easy question to answer, especially if your preference is to work by yourself, however, it is frequently asked during cabin crew final interviews.
- Keep in mind that a key requirement for this job is teamwork.
- Do not answer "It depends on the situation."

SAMPLE ANSWER

"I prefer to work in a group, but I also enjoy having a part of the work that is my personal responsibility."

YOUR ANSWER

26. How would your friends or coworkers describe you?

- Prepare some quotes from your coworkers or friends.
- Stay focused on the skills and traits that are relevant to the cabin crew job.
- Do not get into lengthy stories about your friends or coworkers.

SAMPLE ANSWER

"Both my friends and colleagues would say that I am a reliable individual. They all know that they can count on me to listen to their problems and try to help them find a solution."

or

"John Smith, my colleague at Company A always said that I am the most organized person he knows because my area was always clean and I never left home before tidying up the day's work."

YOUR ANSWER

27. Tell me about a time when you helped someone.

- Be prepared with some examples of situations when you helped either a customer or a colleague.
- Stay focused on the required skills for the cabin crew position.
- Use the names of your colleagues or customers.

SAMPLE ANSWER

"Mrs. Smith, a regular guest in our hotel, had just checked in together with her niece and twin babies. We were not informed that the children would need sleeping cots, so the arrangements were not made. We only had one cot available. I talked to our manager and explained the situation. We ordered a new cot that was delivered on the same day, so I made sure the room was arranged, together with complimentary toys and blankets and the details of the babysitter. Both Mrs. Smith and her niece were very grateful, and my manager praised my efforts."

YOUR ANSWER

28. Tell me about a time you made a suggestion to improve business.

- Talk about the time you gave a suggestion that was further used to benefit the company.
- Do not tell the interviewers about suggestions that were ignored at the time only to be implemented later.
- If this never happened to you, answer honestly and focus instead on the efficiency of the company you work for and how this is achieved.

SAMPLE ANSWER

"In the restaurant I worked we had sugar packs on each table. We were consuming a lot of those packages every week. I suggested to my supervisor that we introduce sugar cubes on the trays when we serve coffee or tea.

Couple of months later, he told me that this change cut the sugar consumption in the restaurant by 30% and many people gave positive feedback regarding the new set up."

YOUR ANSWER

29. Tell me about the most fun you ever experienced on the job.

- Discuss a successful project you enjoyed completing, not the workplace cafeteria pranks.
- Take this chance to reinforce your team player skills.
- Keep the answer short and professional.

SAMPLE ANSWER

"Every December we have a 'sales person of the year' competition. Last year, the sales associates divided into two teams and we had our competition to see who sells the most. We had great fun making daily charts and posting them for everyone to see. We sold so much that month, we became the best selling store."

YOUR ANSWER

30. What techniques and tools do you use to keep yourself organized?

- Refer to tips and techniques that helped you the most, how you acquired those skills and how you taught other people to use them.
- If you never had a job, refer instead to how you kept organized in school.
- Give specific examples.

SAMPLE ANSWER

"I learned that planning is one of the most powerful tools in being efficient. Friday afternoon I list all the tasks for the coming week, as well as the tasks that were not accomplished in the week that passed and should be addressed with priority. I highlight the deadlines and prepare the materials for meetings. I set reminders not only for myself but also for the other team members involved in the projects.

I also use calendar meeting reminders and excel sheets to keep track of my progress."

YOUR ANSWER

31. Give me an example of a time that you felt you went above and beyond the call of duty at work.

- Forget about modesty at this point and get comfortable praising yourself.
- This example has to be an extraordinary thing that you did at work that brought not only you but the entire business or team a great accomplishment.
- Do not include something that you should be doing anyway as per your job description.

SAMPLE ANSWER

"Every year our shop was going through an audit to establish compliance with the company's standards of merchandising. There were four people in our department at that time. We started preparing for the audit and arranging all the products as per the set standard, but it was getting already too late, and my colleagues who finished their shift went home. When my shift was over, not everything was ready for the next day. I asked the floor manager for a couple of more hours to make sure that everything was perfect, but he could not approve the overtime allowance. I had to choose if I stay overtime without being paid, or bring my entire department score lower. Of course, I stayed until everything was exactly as it should have been. Our audit was a success, and I was very proud to have been able to help accomplish this."

YOUR ANSWER

32. What are the steps you follow to study a problem before making a decision?

- With this question, the interviewer wants to find out if you are capable of solving problems or not, and more importantly, if you can avoid common pitfalls.
- This question is asked to establish how you work with your management, employees or customers when things are not clear.
- Stay positive and remember to show your team spirit.

SAMPLE ANSWER

"Before I make a decision I want to make sure that I have as much information as possible. I achieve this by asking people who are involved open-ended questions. If it is not entirely my area of expertise, I ask clarifying details from my colleagues who are responsible for those aspects. If time permits, I run different scenarios with my team and see their reaction and questions that arise. I found that many times this step brought an entirely different perspective and helped me take a correct final decision. Finally, I propose the solution to my manager."

YOUR ANSWER

33. Describe a time when your work was criticized.

- Describe a situation that became a positive lesson you learned.
- Do not get into extensive details about how you felt and how unfair it was to be criticized.
- Keep positive.

SAMPLE ANSWER

"I was in my first weeks working as a barista at ABC Coffee Shop. It was my first experience of this kind, and after my week of initial training, I was assigned at the counter to prepare the drinks. It was rush hour, and the shop got very busy. I tried my best to be as fast as possible, but after my shift, the manager came to me and told me that he knows that I am just at the beginning, but I have to speed up my work and become more efficient. My ego was hurt, but I asked him for practical advice on how I could achieve better results in the future. He was very helpful and gave me a couple of tips - things that I could prepare in advance and make my work easier when the busy time starts. This helped me tremendously, and I learned to be one step ahead."

YOUR ANSWER

34. Explain what has disappointed you most about a previous job?

- Do not get into too many details and do not be too negative.
- As with any other negative question, keep your answer short.
- Go to safe areas such as challenge, responsibilities or furthering your career.

SAMPLE ANSWER

"I left my previous job as a bookkeeper because the environment was monotonous and my career development path would have been very slow if I had stayed in that organization."

YOUR ANSWER

35. What is your greatest failure, and what did you learn from it?

- Give an example of a minor situation that you were able to turn into a positive outcome and a great lesson learned.
- Do not describe a major failure in your career. Do not talk about being let go from a job, unless the interviewer asks specific questions about this subject.
- Do not get personal.

SAMPLE ANSWER

"I was recently promoted to shift manager. We had a tight deadline for one of our most esteemed clients. Things did not work out that good, and we had to extend the delivery date. It was an embarrassing moment as I felt that I failed my company, the client and also my colleagues. When I discussed the matter with my team, I realized they were not even aware of how important it was to finish in time and how tight the deadline was. That is when I understood that I could not expect my team to deliver unless I communicate clearly what the expectations are and motivate them to give their highest performance."

YOUR ANSWER

36. If I were your supervisor and asked you to do something that you disagreed with, what would you do?

- Ask for more information if this question comes up. Would they ask you to do something illegal or it was just something that could have been delegated to somebody else?
- Show that you are willing to go the extra mile for the job, but you still have strong principles.
- Be honest.

SAMPLE ANSWER

"I believe that when you are a good worker, the supervisor will trust you more to assign certain projects knowing that the job will be done right. If the task I would be given interfered with my daily tasks, I will explain this to my manager or suggest another trustworthy colleague.

If it is something that somebody else could do, but my supervisor considered me more appropriate for the job, I will do it."

YOUR ANSWER

37. When were you most satisfied in your job?

- This is a question that refers to when the job brought you joy, not the other way around.
- Specify the skills that you displayed to reach this satisfaction.
- Link this answer to excellent customer service skills if possible.

SAMPLE ANSWER

"I once had a customer with a small child who was very sick and needed constant care and attention. A doctor and a nurse were with them. I expressed my openness to assist, frequently checking with the parents if there was anything we could do to make them and their child more comfortable. In the end, he was happy and smiling, and the parents were very grateful for our attention. That smile from a small boy that didn't have that much to smile about made my day and made me feel that my work and attitude made a difference."

YOUR ANSWER

38. Can you describe a time when you had to be flexible in your job?

- Be prepared with a detailed example for this question.
- Stay away from stories that describe how you had to negotiate company's rules, regulations or code of conduct.
- Being flexible means that you can adjust to a set regulation without ignoring it.

SAMPLE ANSWER

"We once had a guest in our hotel who approached me saying that she loves our bathrobes and would like to keep one. It was not the hotel's policy to allow guests to remove branded items. I approached my manager, and we were able to find a brand new bathrobe and informed the guest that she would be able to purchase it. She was very happy that we could arrange this for her."

YOUR ANSWER

39. Can you describe a situation when you had to take charge?

- Do not give examples of how you took charge and made decisions contradicting your supervisor's or went behind his back.
- Give details about your achievement, but maintain your modesty.
- Do not forget to praise the team you worked with.

SAMPLE ANSWER

"My supervisor was ill, and the store manager asked me to fill in his spot for the day, as we were expecting a visit from the main office. I gathered all my colleagues and explained that our supervisor was not coming in that day and the management asked me to fill in his position. I explained the expectations and asked for their full co-operation and doing their best for the day. Everybody was very supportive, we worked very well as a team, and the visit was a success."

YOUR ANSWER

40. Have you ever had a deadline?

- This is a yes or no question.
- Answer honestly and be prepared to provide an example.
- If you are asked for further details, describe a time you worked as part of a team, and it was successful.

SAMPLE ANSWER

"Yes, I worked in an environment where there were constant deadlines to achieve."

YOUR ANSWER

41. Describe a time you worked as part of a team and it failed due to one or a couple of people.
- Briefly explain the situation, without insisting on who was to blame for the issue.
- Explain what you did to improve the outcome.
- End focusing on the lesson learned, both for you and your colleagues.

SAMPLE ANSWER

"It was Christmas time, and our shop was very busy with the holiday shoppers. We had to make sure there was plenty of merchandise ordered and displayed. Also, all the customers had to be assisted. In the afternoon we found that one of our best selling articles was no longer in stock. Our colleague who was in charge of deliveries did not order the correct amount of items. This put us all in an awkward spot as we had to send the clients to other shops and the sales target was not reached that day. My initial reaction was to be upset with our colleague who made a mistake, but when the manager talked to us, we realized that it could have happened to anybody and instead we should just focus on redirecting our customers and do damage control. That is when we introduced a system of double-checking the orders. I learned then to shift my focus from being upset with the person who made a mistake to finding a solution for the long term and make sure that the mistake has little chance of reoccurrence."

YOUR ANSWER

42. Give me an example of a time when you did not agree with your supervisor. What was it and what did you do?

- Keep the subject light and do not get into too many details.
- Do not insist too much on the cause of the disagreement and the emotions involved, but rather on how you reached a consensus.
- End on a positive note.

SAMPLE ANSWER

"We were implementing a new accounting software in my department. During the test period, my manager wanted to run both the old and the new system until everybody was trained on the new one. That meant double input from the people who were already trained. I approached him and explained that the double workload would be difficult to manage, but he did not want to change his mind. He told me that there is no other way to work both platforms at the same time. I approached our IT department who were aware of this issue, and within a couple of days, they were ready with a solution to run both programs on one database but inputs from both the old and the new software. I went to my supervisor, and I presented him with the suggestion. He was pleased with my initiative."

YOUR ANSWER

43. Describe a time when you had to deal with conflicting demands.

- Only discuss how you successfully dealt with the issue, reinforcing your problem-solving skills and your ability to prioritize.
- Do not discuss poor management decisions or talk badly about your co-workers or manager.
- Do not give out more information than you should.

SAMPLE ANSWER

"I was fulfilling my weekly task of checking the merchandise stock and writing the next order. In the same time, my shift manager asked me to come in the store and train the new colleagues in the product placement standards. I approached my manager and told her that I was in the middle of my inventory and I would not be able to come, but she insisted that I do it immediately. I had to postpone my work, so I asked one of my senior colleagues to help me in checking the stocks, and I would fill in the estimates for the next order later. I also managed to finish the training faster by demonstrating the correct procedure and then supervising my colleagues in creating one or two displays. Everything was sorted out, and I managed to send my order by the day's end."

YOUR ANSWER

44. Do you have any blind spots?

- This is a trick question. If you had blind spots, you would not be aware of them.
- Try to make yourself look good and do not admit to failings. A failing is not a blind spot.
- Keep your answers neutral, short and professional.

SAMPLE ANSWER

"When things come to my attention, I make an effort to improve myself and become better at my job. I listen to questions and constructive criticism at work, as I believe it will bring self-awareness and encourages an open communication environment."

YOUR ANSWER

45. Describe a time you were faced with a customer of a different background, and you had to change the way you communicated and behaved towards them.

- Keep the subject light.
- Be respectful of all cultures and backgrounds, especially when they are different from yours.
- The interviewers want to see that you are capable of adjusting your behavior and service delivery to meet the customer's needs and expectations without breaching company values.
- Do not make any comments about religious beliefs, language abilities or specific behaviors.

SAMPLE ANSWER

"I was serving a traditional Arabic family that came to our restaurant. When I went to take the order, I noticed that the lady did not address me and the order was given by her husband. To make the woman more comfortable, I asked one of my female colleagues to take over serving her, while I would serve the gentleman. I could see that she was immediately relaxed and interacted with my colleague. The supervisor told me that even though we had to shift some of my fellow team members and reassign their work, this was the best solution and congratulated me for the initiative."

YOUR ANSWER

46. Give me an example of a situation when you had to be diplomatic to your customer.

- Show you can maintain a positive attitude even when under pressure.
- Discuss your ability to use active listening and open communication with the customer.
- Remember: "Rule 1: The customer is always right. Rule 2: If the customer is ever wrong, re-read Rule 1."

SAMPLE ANSWER

"We had a couple dining at our restaurant. One of them was talking extremely loud, and we received complaints from the other patrons. I went to him and asked if he had a good time and if he is pleased with our service. He was very content with his dinner and server. I asked him to kindly use a lower tone in their conversation as we could all hear what they were talking about. He said he did not realize that he was talking so loud and thanked me for bringing it to his attention."

YOUR ANSWER

47. Give me an example of a situation when you had to say no to the customer.
- Diplomacy is your biggest ally while answering this question.
- Focus on the innovative ways you found to compensate for the "no" you had to say to the customer, rather than the reaction of the customer.
- Do not criticize or comment on the customer's demands.

SAMPLE ANSWER

"On of the customers in our restaurant told me she liked our salt and pepper shakers and she will pay whatever amount we ask as long as could she take home a set. I told her that it was not possible as it was against the policy; however, I volunteer to find out the place where she could buy them. I talked to my manager, and we obtained the name and address of our supplier. She was very pleased with this solution."

YOUR ANSWER

48. Give me an example of a situation when you did something extra for your customer. What was it?

- Do not be modest - this is an excellent opportunity to praise yourself.
- Make sure that you showcase a skill that is required for the cabin crew position.
- Describe in detail the reaction of the customer and highlight the impact that your action had over the relationship between the business and the customer.

SAMPLE ANSWER

"We had a mother with two children shopping in our store. They were quite active, running around and the mother seemed quite uncomfortable. I approached her and asked if while she took her time to look and maybe tried some items from our new collection, I may show the children around as we were preparing our new holiday-themed window display. She agreed, and I spent some time explaining to the kids how we dress the mannequins and how we make the decorations for the windows. The mother was amazed to find her children absorbed in inspecting the different types of stars that we were planning to use. A couple of days later, my manager received a wonderful email from her explaining how special she felt and how her kids were taken care of without her asking anything from us. She described how precious it was for a busy mom to be offered half an hour in a shop just to browse around. I was delighted that I could do that for her."

YOUR ANSWER

49. What are your strengths?

- The interviewer expects you to give examples of how you excelled in your previous jobs.
- Prepare 4 or 5 traits that are relevant to the cabin crew position and be also prepared to give examples of when you displayed these strengths.
- Talk about your strengths in the area of customer service, teamwork, communication, attention to detail or problem-solving.
- Do not discuss your strengths outside the work area.

SAMPLE ANSWER

"I am a team player with excellent attention to detail. I provide personalized service to my customers while aiming to go beyond all expectations and ensure they receive the best possible service. I also can quickly adjust in a fast-paced environment."

YOUR ANSWER

50. What are your weaknesses?

- Do not give information which could hurt your professional image or decrease your chances of getting the job.
- Disclose a weakness only when you have already taken steps to compensate for it.
- Do not say that you have no weaknesses.

SAMPLE ANSWER

"I feel that my attention to detail is my weakness. I want everything to be perfect. Sometimes I get so caught up in small details that I forget to see the big picture. It was pointed to me in the past, and I am striving to improve myself. I am now always finding ways to balance both the details and the overall situation."

YOUR ANSWER

51. Tell me about a time when you had to deal with a co-worker who wasn't doing his/her fair share of the work. What did you do and what was the outcome?

- Keep your answer professional, diplomatic, short and clear.
- Focus more on what you did to deal with the situation, rather than how much you were bothered by your colleague not doing their work.
- Turn your answer into a positive experience.

SAMPLE ANSWER

"Sofia was my shift colleague. During lunch service, I saw her being slow to take orders and attend to the new customers. I had to step in her area and do part of her work. After the service was over, I asked her what was happening. I learned that her grandmother was ill and she just received the news that morning. I helped her out for the next days until she felt better. She appreciated my willingness to do something for her and we are now working very well together, taking extra work from each other whenever is necessary."

YOUR ANSWER

52. Give me an example of a time you did something wrong. How did you handle it?

- An honest answer to this question shows that you are not afraid to admit when you are wrong, however, do not bring up examples of gross misconduct or disappointing performance.
- Focus not on what you did wrong, but the steps that followed to correct your mistake.
- Summarize what you learned from the experience.

SAMPLE ANSWER

"I was working as a hostess at ABC Restaurant, and my duties included handling the reservations. One day, I took a reservation for the evening when the entire restaurant was fully booked. I realized this only later when we were preparing for the dinner service. I approached the restaurant manager and explained my mistake. He approved one more table to be set up on top of our arrangement. This way we were able to accommodate everybody. I apologized to my manager, and he was very understanding and told me that for any problem, there is a solution. I took that along, and no matter what happens, I will always search for a viable resolve for any issues that may arise."

YOUR ANSWER

53. Describe how you would handle a situation if you were required to finish multiple tasks by the end of the day, and there was no conceivable way that you could finish them.

- This question is asked to establish if you are capable of setting realistic priorities for your work.
- Do not say that you will do all in your power to finish the work, this is not the point.
- Be clear and concise in your answer and offer a solution.

SAMPLE ANSWER

"There are two possible ways I would handle this. Firstly, I will solve the tasks that I could realistically do myself and set aside the tasks that I could ask help from colleagues or my supervisor. If that would not be possible, I will make a list of the tasks in order of importance, and I will handle each of them, starting with the most urgent. I would also be trying to establish which duties can be postponed for the following day. I will inform my manager before I start this and try to get his advice on how I can handle it better."

YOUR ANSWER

54. Tell me about a time you misjudged a person.

- Use an example where you underestimated somebody, rather than an example when you thought that someone was trustworthy and in the end, they disappointed you.
- End your answer with a summary of what you learned from the experience.

SAMPLE ANSWER

"Our office assistant was a timid and reserved person. One day I started to talk to him, and I found out that he was an engineer in his country, but came here to provide a safer future for his children. He was doing the job to learn the language better and understand our culture. We became friends, and sometimes he was offering his input with some of the projects I was working on. I told to my manager his story, and after some time, we had an opening which he interviewed for. Now he is working in the planning department. I learned to never judge somebody by the job they are doing and just stay curious."

YOUR ANSWER

55. What's the most difficult decision you've made in the last two years and how did you come to that decision?

- Relate this answer strictly to your professional life.
- Talk about how you changed your job or major to do something you are passionate about.
- Do not talk negatively about your former colleagues or manager.
- End on a positive note with the lesson you've learned from the experience.

SAMPLE ANSWER

"I have been working at ABC Company for three years as a Personal Assistant to the General Manager. I liked the job, but I missed working with customers and meeting more people. In a fragile economy, I decided to change my career and look for employment in the hospitality business. Because I did not have experience, I was offered a starter job in the housekeeping department of a reputable hotel. It was hard work, but after one year was promoted two times and eventually got a position working as a junior housekeeping manager. I met and assisted interesting people from all over the world, and I was very happy with what I achieved. It was a tough decision to take, but it eventually led me to where I am today."

YOUR ANSWER

56. Tell me about a challenge at work you faced and overcame recently.

- Talk about the complaints you solved, issues you had to organize or conflicts you had to resolve.
- Focus on the problem-solving, not on the problem itself.
- Do not put anybody else in a bad light.

SAMPLE ANSWER

"We received a new computer software that would take the reservations for the day, in addition to the customer details, orders, and home-delivery schedule. It took a long time to input all the data while the customers were waiting on the line. I asked the manager to approve my training from the IT department. In only 30 minutes they taught me all the shortcuts, and I managed to be efficient when operating it."

YOUR ANSWER

57. How are you planning to establish credibility with the members of your team?

- Talk about your ability to integrate into a group and the skills that might assist you to get the job done.
- Reinforce that the team success is as important to you as personal success.
- Do not say that people have to consider you knowledgeable because you have the highest education or broadest experience.

SAMPLE ANSWER

"A team expects from a new member to have the ability to improve their efforts. I am dedicated to helping my teammates complete the work, and I strive to achieve a common goal. I am open to learning how the team operates and I will listen to the advice and criticism that will be given to me. I will offer my experience and knowledge, and I will do the best I can to become a valuable part of the operation."

YOUR ANSWER

58. Tell me about a time you resolved a conflict.

- This question is asked to showcase how you deal with a possible difference of opinion that may arise in the aircraft.
- Talk about a specific example when you excelled at solving a conflict.
- Do not talk about personal relationships with bosses or co-workers.

SAMPLE ANSWER

"Two of the sales associates in my team were having a hard time getting along. The work has been delegated at the beginning of the week, and Amy was in charge of the inventory, while Karen had to re-arrange the display. Each of them was interfering with the other person's work. After I had talked to both of them, I found out that Amy was interested in the artistic part of the job, while Karen was studying accounting and was fascinated by bookkeeping. I explained to each of them how their issues were affecting the business as a whole. They understood and apologized to each other. I also realized that delegating tasks like these might not be the best approach. Since then, I ask the associates to volunteer for the specific duties. I found that this way people are more motivated to do the job they love and are interested in."

YOUR ANSWER

59. Have you worked with someone you didn't like? If so, how did you handle it?
- This is a trick question.
- Speaking negatively about other people will show you as an unreliable colleague.
- Stay professional and be diplomatic.

SAMPLE ANSWER

"Not really. I believe that when disagreements occur, the matters can be taken up with the concerned person in a polite and considerate manners and be immediately solved. "

YOUR ANSWER

60. What sorts of people do you enjoy working with?

- Talk about your ability to smoothly and efficiently work in a team and be aware of improving yourself and your skill set.
- Discuss the times when you and your team managed customer complaints or projects which ended up being successful.
- Do not bring up race, class, religion, gender or other similar issues and do not discuss how sometimes it's difficult to work with your colleagues.

SAMPLE ANSWER

"I believe that there is something valuable to learn from every single person I encounter.

Once, I had a family who was just checking out and they had some issues with their room service. I asked the food and beverage manager to come and address the complaint. He was courteous, empathetic and proactive. He listened to the customers and acknowledged their concerns. He successfully turned the situation around, and the guests were delighted with his solution. I watched the dialogue, and I learned more about excellent customer service. In the end, I told my colleague that I admired the way he handled the situation. I love working with people like him."

YOUR ANSWER

61. What is the kind of person you refuse to work with?
- This is a trick question.
- Airlines are multicultural, multilingual, multinational companies. Stay focused on how you are capable of learning something from everybody and on your willingness to be part of such a team.
- Never admit there is a type of person you will refuse to work with unless that kind of person is a detriment to the company and its policies.

SAMPLE ANSWER

"I can work with all kinds of individuals. I believe that everybody has an interesting story to tell and something to teach me."

YOUR ANSWER

62. What kind of situation do you find stressful?

- Express your belief that being under pressure is just an opportunity to overcome a challenge and deliver excellence.
- Give an example of a stressful situation and talk about how you successfully handled the customer demands while being under pressure.
- Do not talk about problems with your coworkers or managers and do not badmouth your employer.

SAMPLE ANSWER

"We had hectic weekends at the restaurant where I was working as a hostess. My job was to show people to their table and present the menus, answer the phone, manage the reservations book and trying to accommodate the customers who came in without a reservation. I was striving to do everything, rushing with the new clients so I can pick up the phone and go the extra mile to accommodate the customers without a reservation. I felt exhausted and decided that perhaps I was not very efficient in my approach. I decided to prioritize and take my time and show the new patrons their tables and discussing the specials and the menu options. I talked to my manager and the times when I could not answer the phone; it was arranged that the call was redirected towards a voicemail where the customer would leave his name, and contact number and the desired timing of the reservation and I would return their call to confirm when the restaurant was less busy. This way I managed to offer personalized service and still be efficient in my work."

YOUR ANSWER

63. Would you say that you can easily deal with high-pressure situations?
- Explain your ability to work under pressure, without describing with too much detail why you thought a particular situation was stressful.
- The cabin crew job is a high-pressure work environment, so do not say that you can't work well under pressure.
- Do not spend too much time discussing the amount of high stress in everyday life.
    SAMPLE ANSWER
"Yes. I have been dealing with busy times in the restaurant. There is always pressure for the service to be completed in time. It motivates me to work faster and find innovative ways to be more efficient."
    YOUR ANSWER

64. Describe a situation where you had to make a quick decision.

- This question is asked to establish if you have the ability to think about problems before they arise.
- Give examples of successful decision making on your job.
- Keep your answers professional and relevant.

SAMPLE ANSWER

"I was working at the ABC Restaurant. We were preparing for a big event. Before any of my colleagues arrived at work, I was handling supplies delivery, when I realized that the supplier did not bring us all the necessary items. Oil and vinegar were missing from the list, and what we had left in the pantry was not sufficient. I decided to immediately drive to the nearest supermarket and buy the necessary quantity. Later, I explained to my supervisor what happened, and he was pleased with my initiative."

YOUR ANSWER

65. What do you enjoy the most about working with customers?

- Avoid the standard answer "I enjoy meeting new people every day."
- Talk about the satisfaction you get from dealing with your customers.
- Address emotional issues. You are aiming for the interviewer to be moved by your drive and dedication.

SAMPLE ANSWER

"I like to feel that I made somebody's day with something I did or a small detail added to my service. I enjoy seeing people relaxing and having a good time. Mostly I am very proud when people tell me that it is the best service they received in a long time."

YOUR ANSWER

66. When could your customer service have been better?

- This question is asked to establish if you have the ability to recognize when your service delivery might need improvement, as well as the integrity to admit there is always room to perform better.
- Bring up a minor incident and offer an explanation on how you realized your mistake and solved it, without the customer being impacted.
- Do not talk about instances when you completely failed to deliver excellent customer service, regardless of the reason.

SAMPLE ANSWER

"The policy in our restaurant was to welcome the guests and offer a basket of bread, butter, and olives while waiting for the drinks and food to be ready. We had a customer who came often, and I served him many times. I knew he was always asking for brown bread instead of white, and typically I was serving him straight away the brown bread. This day I was distracted with other customers and forgot about his preference. He had to call me back to remind me of the brown bread. I apologized and told him I remembered his request from his previous visits and I would fulfill it immediately. I realized then that excellent service is in the small details, no matter how busy or caught up I am in my work."

YOUR ANSWER

67. Give an example of excellent customer service that you experienced as a customer.

- This question is asked to establish that you can recognize superior customer service from others.
- Do not be afraid to praise other people.
- If possible, try to give examples in the aviation environment - in the aircraft, ticketing office or airport. Otherwise, talk about your experience in restaurants, cafes, or other hospitality establishments.

SAMPLE ANSWER

"I was going on vacation with my sister. At the check-in desk in the airport, there was a lady who greeted us with a smile, addressed to us by our names and asked for our seat preference. She even noticed that for our connecting flight we did not have seats together and sent a message to that airport. We got to sit together all the way to our destination. She was polite, friendly, attentive, gave us personalized service and attention. She foresaw a potential problem in our experience and immediately solved it. I still remember her. When we were on the plane, we wrote a recommendation letter to the airline."

YOUR ANSWER

68. Give an example of excellent customer service you provided.
- Talk about going above and beyond the call of the job. Do not be shy.
- Give the full story of how pleased your customers were and exactly what you did to accomplish that.
- Talk about the reaction of your colleagues or supervisor.

SAMPLE ANSWER

"I was working in a department store, and I had a customer, an elderly lady who was looking to buy a wallet. The store was on seven levels and not very easy to navigate. I offered to escort the lady myself to the counter where she could find what she was looking for. I helped her out in choosing one, explaining what the difference between them, the country where they were produced and the type of leather used. She said that nobody takes the time nowadays and everybody is in a rush to sell. She was extremely pleased that I took my time and showed her the way to the right floor as well as helping her find the exact wallet she wanted. In the end, she gave me a hug and every time she stopped by the store she came to say hello to me."

YOUR ANSWER

69. How can you deal with an upset guest in the plane?

- Emphasize your customer service skills such as active listening, empathy and problem-solving.
- Think about the fact that you are in the air, with limited access to resources.
- This is a hypothetical question, and you should be creative, but do not overdo it by offering solutions that you cannot possibly fulfill.

SAMPLE ANSWER

"I believe that the most challenging aspect of customer service in the plane is the limited resources that we have available. Therefore, I would use my soft skills and listen to the customer's complaint, use positive body language and open-ended questions. I would ask him to give me a solution to solve his issue, and to the best of my ability and following the airline's policies I will try to fulfill it. I would keep on checking on him throughout the flight to make sure that he is happy and feels taken care of."

YOUR ANSWER

70. If I spoke to your boss, what would she say are your strengths and weaknesses?

- Mention three or four strengths relevant for the cabin crew position and one minor weakness.
- Do not start to elaborate your answer.
- Make sure that you also prepare an additional response that includes how you are addressing your weakness, shall the recruiter follow the question with this topic.

SAMPLE ANSWER

"She would tell you that I am a dedicated employee, eager to learn and be the best in my job, a good listener and an organized person.

She will also mention that my attention to detail sometimes takes priority over the big picture and that has an impact on my efficiency."

YOUR ANSWER

71. What do you expect from a supervisor?
- Be specific and give a couple of traits you appreciate in a manager.
- Focus on team spirit and integrity.
- Do not start talking negatively about your previous supervisors.

SAMPLE ANSWER

"I expect her to offer guidance and support. I also appreciate a supervisor who is fair, honest and encourages the professional development of each person in the team."

YOUR ANSWER

72. Do you think a manager should be feared or liked?

- This is a trick question. Managers and subordinates do not need to be friends to achieve the goals of the company.
- During the job interview, do not mention any negative aspects - no matter how trivial, about your previous managers.
- Do not give example and keep your answer short and professional.

SAMPLE ANSWER

"I think it is not important whether a manager is feared or liked. What matters is that the manager is capable and fair and she promotes what is the best for the company, for the employees and also for the customers. I know that managers sometimes have to make tough calls which are not agreed by all."

YOUR ANSWER

73. What motivates you to do the best on the job?

- This is a trick question.
- You want to show the assessors that you are self-motivated when it comes to your work.
- Do not answer that salary, travel benefits or cabin crew lifestyle are your motivators.

SAMPLE ANSWER

"I always felt that it is important both for the company and for me personally to provide excellent service and have extremely satisfied customers every day. This is my biggest motivator."

YOUR ANSWER

74. If you had to choose one, would you consider yourself a big-picture person or a detail-oriented person?

- There is no right or wrong answer.
- Try to incorporate both traits, but express your preference for one or the other.
- Elaborate your answer, do not give only a one-liner.

SAMPLE ANSWER

"At the core, I am a detail oriented person. I used to be so attentive to details that I did not consider things to be acceptable until all the small aspects were perfected. Meanwhile, I understood that this might not be the most efficient approach, so I am making an effort to consider the overall picture. I am doing this without cutting back on the quality of service or products I deliver."

YOUR ANSWER

75. How would you describe your work style?

- Your work style is a combination of skills, knowledge, and personality traits that determine how you approach job functions.
- Talk about how you communicate with others, what is your approach to deadlines and problem-solving techniques.
- Make sure the answer showcases your strengths.

SAMPLE ANSWER

"I take my job very seriously. I enjoy the fast paced environment in which I work and the unique challenges. Together with my team, we strive to find the fastest and most efficient solution to the issues that arise every day."

YOUR ANSWER

76. What is your communication style?

- It takes a lot of self-awareness to be able to see your communication style.
- Talk about how you tend to solve a conflict, what type of verbal communication you prefer and what do you believe in.
- Emphasize an assertive communication style.

SAMPLE ANSWER

"I think that everybody has something valuable to say, so I strive to always listen to the other person's point of view. I am using simple, easy to understand language and I encourage people to ask me if something I say is not clear. I believe the majority of people have good intentions, and if there were a mistake made, I would look for solutions rather than find somebody to blame for the error. I have been told by my managers and colleagues that I am enthusiastic and motivating."

YOUR ANSWER

77. Do you like to work by yourself or in a team?

- You are interviewing for a cabin crew position. The most important skill for this job is the ability to work well in a team.
- Talk about the benefits of working with others.
- Do not say that you prefer working solo.

SAMPLE ANSWER

"I prefer to work together with other people. I think that every member of the team has a unique talent which will be showcased when the person is dedicated to doing the best he can do on his own. Superior results, however, will be achieved only by having more people contributing towards the same goal."

YOUR ANSWER

78. How do you like to work with your supervisor?

- This is one of the most asked questions during an interview.
- It is asked to establish if your work style matches the company values regarding cabin crew - management relation.
- Do not say that you prefer minimum input from your supervisor.

SAMPLE ANSWER

"I like to work with a manager who communicates clearly his expectations and the goals of the project we are working on. I prefer somebody who leads by example and is involved together with the team to accomplish the task at hand."

YOUR ANSWER

79. List five words that describe your character.

- Make sure you mention character traits that are relevant to the flight attendant job.
- Do not be reserved in praising yourself. Be honest.
- If you're not sure how to answer this question, ask your closest friends how would they describe you.

SAMPLE ANSWER
"I am reliable, optimistic, a good listener, problem-solver and passionate about continuous learning."

YOUR ANSWER

80. Do you plan your day?

- People who start their day having a plan, get more done than the people who just go with the flow.
- Bring up how you focus on getting things done in order of importance.
- Talk only about day planning in the workplace.

SAMPLE ANSWER

"Yes. I start my day at 8:30AM with a meeting with the rest of the department where the daily goals are discussed. After the meeting, I focus on my daily agenda, starting with the tasks that are most urgent and important or the tasks that were not solved from the previous day. I like to take care of the important clients early, to make sure I have plenty of time to address their queries, shall they arise. At the end of the day, I summarize my activity and make a list of what I need to do the next day."

YOUR ANSWER

81. What will you miss about your present job?

- By asking this question, the interviewer wants to know that you can map out the differences between your current job and the cabin crew job.
- Do not say that you will not miss anything about your current job.
- Do not be overly sad about what you leave behind.

SAMPLE ANSWER

"I will miss my colleagues. We are a very tight team, and we grew together from new recruits with no experience to a motivated group achieving consistently high performance."

YOUR ANSWER

82. What are your career growth goals with us?

- Talk about your professional five-year plan with the company and how you are planning to achieve it.
- Do not talk how the job of cabin crew with the airline may eventually get you another job in the private jet airlines or a higher position with your current employer.
- Keep your answers short and straightforward.

SAMPLE ANSWER

"I am aiming to learn how to deliver the best customer service in Economy Class as well as Business and First Class. I am very passionate about self-development and performance management and eventually I would like to have a supervisory role in the aircraft, and perhaps a part-time training position."

YOUR ANSWER

83. Who is your hero? Why?

- Do some research before the interview and choose someone who had an impact in your field.
- This question is asked to establish your personal beliefs and ambitions.
- Do not choose people who are in the gossip tabloids or people who are religious figures. Also, make sure you do not mention someone who is one of the airline's competitors.

SAMPLE ANSWER

"My hero is Steve Jobs because he had a distinct vision about the products he designed. He created the most famous brand in the world by being focused on simplicity and a unique customer service. Moreover, he never gave up his dream."

YOUR ANSWER

84. Describe your motivation for going to the college or university you attended.

- Focus on the training you received in college and its benefit to achieving your professional goals. Discuss the events or clubs you attended.
- Talk about learning social skills necessary to operate in the business world.
- Don't say you chose your school based on the best party school. You do not want to display poor decision making at this stage of the interview.
- If you don't know why you chose a particular school, research any ties it may have to the aviation or hospitality business and discuss those links.

SAMPLE ANSWER

"I chose ABC University because it has one of the oldest, most famous Hotel and Hospitality Management degrees in the United States. During my studies, I was able to complete an internship at XYZ Resort in Bahamas where I learned the practical aspects and incredibly complex insights of running a hotel. For three months I worked at the front desk, housekeeping, food and beverage, guest relations and sales departments, giving me a glimpse on every detail that makes into a successful business. The school also organized an excellent job exhibition at the end of the year. That is where I learned about your airline."

YOUR ANSWER

85. What is the most important thing you learned in school?

- You should talk about the knowledge and skills gained through your education that applies to the cabin crew job and your professional goals.
- Do not give details on your grades or other personal aspects.

SAMPLE ANSWER

"The most important thing I learned is how to be organized and prepare in advance. At the end of each semester we had six exams to take. It was a lot of information to take in, and I learned that the earlier I started with the preparation for my exams, the more successful was the outcome and the lesser my stress level."

YOUR ANSWER

86. Why did you choose your major?

- Stay positive and talk only about your accomplishments. If your major was not your first choice, do not mention that.
- Keep your answer short and neutral.
- Because the education requirement for cabin crew is high school only, this question might lead to the next question *"Your resume suggests that you may be overqualified or too experienced for this position. What is your opinion?"*

SAMPLE ANSWER

"I chose my major because it provided me the skills and knowledge to successfully achieve my career goals."

YOUR ANSWER

87. Your resume suggests that you may be over-qualified or too experienced for this position. What is your opinion?

- Emphasize your interest in establishing a long-term association with the airline.
- Observe that experienced people are always a premium.
- Suggest that since you are so well qualified, the employer will get a fast return on their investment.

SAMPLE ANSWER

"I assume that when performing well on the job, new opportunities will open for me. I believe that a strong company needs strong staff. A growing and visionary airline such as ABC Airways can never have too much talent!"

YOUR ANSWER

88. How do you want to improve yourself in the next year?

- Talk only about your career goals, and mention how you will achieve the next steps towards it.
- Do not talk about hobbies or interests that are not directly related to your professional life.
- Do not give personal information that you wish you had not revealed.

SAMPLE ANSWER

"I would like to pursue an aviation security course. This has been a dream of mine for quite some time. Also, I would like to take a beginner Arabic language course. I believe this will help me in better understanding the life in Dubai, as well as my future customers."

YOUR ANSWER

89. If you had enough money to stop working right now, would you?
- This is a hypothetical question, and as much as honesty is appreciated, a yes answer might bring a different image than the one you are aiming for.
- Do not start talking about how much money is enough money.
- Reinforce your passion for a cabin crew career.

SAMPLE ANSWER

"Having enough money is quite a relative concept. I appreciate a steady income, but that you can get from any job. I want to become a flight attendant because it will be broadening my mind and teach me about other cultures. I also want to learn to deliver the 5-star customer service that your company is well known for."

YOUR ANSWER

90. Do you have any language abilities that might assist you in performing this job?
- Mention only the languages you are confident about at conversational level.
- When answering this question, do not consider language courses you took in high school or during one semester in college.
- Be honest; you never know what languages the person in front of you can speak.

SAMPLE ANSWER

"I am born in an American-Swedish family, so I spoke at home English and Swedish, and I am proficient in both. I also took some Spanish classes; however, I am just a beginner in this language."

YOUR ANSWER

91. Do you have any restrictions on your ability to travel?

- A career as a flight attendant means plenty of travel. You should know this when applying for the job.
- You will be away from home sometimes for a week at a time. If you are a family-oriented person and do not want to be away for extended periods, this is probably not the job for you.
- If for any other reason, you are unable to travel to certain countries, now it's the time to say so.

SAMPLE ANSWER

"I am passionate about travel, and this is why I applied to be a flight attendant. I have no restrictions on my ability to travel anywhere in the world."

YOUR ANSWER

92. Do you need additional training?

- Be honest. If this is your first job as a cabin crew, you might feel that you need additional training in specific airline customer service approach or other areas that might be of benefit to you.
- If you are already a cabin crew, explain your desire to learn more in the field of aviation and deepen your already existing knowledge.
- Think of this as an opportunity to expand your qualifications and add to your skills.

SAMPLE ANSWER

"I feel confident that I will be able to apply the knowledge gained through the regular initial training your airline offers for the tailored service and customer service policies.

As this is my first time working in a multi-cultural company, I think I might benefit from learning more about cultural diversity in such an environment."

YOUR ANSWER

93. How will you be able to cope working such long shifts?

- You will be required to operate flights that can be up to 14 hours long. Your duty can start at 2 AM or 9 PM.
- Focus on how you deal with tiredness and stress.
- End on a positive note.

SAMPLE ANSWER

"I like the fact that even though the shifts are long, there will be enough days off to recover. I have been working six days a week from 9 to 5, and I am looking forward to having more flexibility with my time.

I also started running two years ago and found that it significantly improved my resistance."

YOUR ANSWER

94. How long do you expect to work for us if hired?

- This is the moment to talk about beginning a career with the airline. Talk about your career goals and your long-term plans.
- Do not discuss planning to work with the airline just until you get enough experience to be hired by a bigger airline.
- Keep it short and do not be specific. Otherwise, you put an expiry date on your career plans with them.

SAMPLE ANSWER

"I worked for my previous employer for five years. This demonstrates that I am a loyal person. I plan to grow, learn and improve myself continuously and I will be happy to work as long as possible in an environment that keeps me challenged."

YOUR ANSWER

95. What did you do to prepare for this interview?

- This is a perfect opportunity to tell them about the concerns you've had and what have you been doing to address them.
- You want to come up as somebody who has researched not only the job but also the airline and the aviation industry in general.
- Nobody wants to hear that you just rolled out of bed and showed up at the interview hoping for the best.

SAMPLE ANSWER

"I have been reading the aviation news online, and I subscribed to your airline's newsletter. I've also done some research on the life in Abu Dhabi and the work life of flight attendants."

YOUR ANSWER

96. How would you react if we asked you to change your appearance to fit in with our company?

- Remember that the flight attendant image is a full uniform, from the makeup to the hair, manicure and the way you carry yourself.
- Ask the interviewers to give you an example so you can see what they mean by this question.
- If they expect you to abide by the strict grooming regulations, that is a legitimate question. If however, they want you to color your hair in a particular color, then it is up to you to decide if it is something you consider doing.

SAMPLE ANSWER

"I admire your flight attendants and their polished appearance, and I am sure I will have no difficulties in complying with the airline's grooming requirements."

YOUR ANSWER

97. Which is more important to you, the money or the work?

- This is a trick question. As a principle, work should always be more important than the money.
- Interviewers want to know you consider the work you are doing valuable.
- Try not to seem desperate, even if you need the job for the salary.

SAMPLE ANSWER

"I appreciate my work above all else; however, I expect to be fairly compensated for my contribution."

YOUR ANSWER

98. What advice would you give to someone who was applying to become Cabin Crew?

- The interviewers want to know what is your approach to the process of becoming a cabin crew.
- Give a couple of brief points about how the application process worked for you.
- Be honest and enthusiastic.

SAMPLE ANSWER

"If somebody would apply for the flight attendant position for the first time, I would advise them to take time and build their CV properly. Even if it is their first job, I would suggest they volunteer or participate in internships to give them the customer service experience that is a great advantage. Also, I would encourage them to take high-quality photos and prepare as much as possible for the assessment day."

YOUR ANSWER

99. Are you applying for any other airlines? What if more than one airline offers you the job?
- Make sure that your answer stays professional and diplomatic.
- Be honest, but keep it short.
- Keep your focus on the airline you interview for and what you can do for them.

SAMPLE ANSWER

"I will consider all the factors in my decision making, and I will choose the employer which best fits my career aspirations. Your airline seems to be such a place for me."

YOUR ANSWER

100. Why should we hire you?

- This is the time to sell yourself! It is all about how you fit into the position, not how the position fits with you.
- Talk about your skills and strengths that will benefit the company.
- Do not be general or desperate and answer with: "Because I need a job" or "I think it could be a nice to travel for free." This question is not about what the airline can do for you; it is about what you can do for them.

SAMPLE ANSWER

"You should hire me because I have the expertise and experience in the area of customer service. I aim for excellence in everything I do, and I will give my full energy to achieve outstanding service for your clients. I have reached and exceeded all my targets and customer expectations in my previous job by offering personalized care, attention to details and upbeat energy in my work."

YOUR ANSWER

101. Do you have any questions for me?

- This question is asked because the interviewers want to see you showing interest in getting the job with them.
- Once again, the key here is researching the airline beforehand.
- This is also a good point to ask for feedback on your performance, as well as contact details of the recruitment team.

SAMPLE ANSWER

"I would like to know what does the airline value the most?"

or

"What is the most important thing that I should do to contribute in my first months of flying?"

or

"How do you think I performed during the assessment?"

YOUR ANSWER

Important points about the Final Interview

↪Answer the questions to the point. There is no need to elaborate more than necessary.
↪If the situation described does not apply to you, tell the interviewer that you were never faced with such a scenario.
↪Do not reveal information that you do not want your potential employer to know about you.
↪Be prepared with answers and examples for all the questions that might come up.
↪If the answer does not come immediately to you, take a moment to think about it and tell the interviewer you need time to think.
↪Be honest.
↪Be extremely diplomatic in your answers.
↪Use simple language.
↪Be aware of your body language throughout the discussion.
↪Do not talk negatively about your current or past employer or colleagues.
↪Ask the interviewer for their contact information and etiquette for being in touch (when should you contact them, what method do they prefer - email, phone, etc).

2.3 AFTER THE ASSESSMENT

Now that the difficult part is over, the excruciating part is about to begin: the waiting period. The next 4-6 weeks (sometimes even longer) will be the longest weeks of your life. You will go through every single detail of the interview. You will be feeling confident, just to be full of doubt 5 minutes later. It's an emotional roller coaster. An answer will come soon, so try to keep sane meanwhile.
Successful candidates will receive a phone call, while the ones who did not make it will receive an email.

2.3.1 GOLDEN CALL AND SUCCESSFUL CANDIDATE EMAIL

Your phone will start ringing, and there will be this long number starting with +97. Deep down you know this is it and you start either jumping and be overwhelmed with happiness, or you completely freeze. Whichever your reaction, try to pick up the phone and listen to the good news.

Do not worry about how you are perceived at this point; it is natural to be speechless or full of joy. Some people even start crying. The bottom line is this: You made it! Congratulations!!!

The airline representative will tell you that you will be receiving an email with instructions in the following days.

2.3.2 DOCUMENT SUBMISSION

Once you receive your instructions email, the real work starts.

There will be complex medical examinations that you must complete before joining. You will be tested, checked and measured in more detail than ever before. You should not resign from your current job at this point. Your offer of employment is not final until you passed all the required medical tests.

Medical documents
Some of the medical tests include:
- HIV test
- Full blood count
- Hepatitis B and C test
- Detailed chest X-ray report about heart and lungs
- Cervical smear test report
- Audiogram report and graph
- Eye test (regardless if you wear glasses or not)
- Dental Certificate
- Vaccination Card
- General health assessment Certificate

The medical tests are different for each employer, and you should not start them before you receive the full instructions from the airline.

Every single medical report will then be scanned and submitted to the airline via the careers portal, or email.

I recommend you see your family doctor first. In some countries (Europe, Canada, etc.), when referred to by the family physician, part of the cost of your tests will be covered by your insurance or national health scheme.

Otherwise, expect to pay for these tests. Whatever the amount is, it will not be reimbursed by the airline.

Other documents
You will also have to send:
- The contract signed on every single page.

- Copies of birth certificates for you and your family members.
- Passport copies for you and your family members.
- Education certificates.
- Copies of your licenses (if you have previous cabin crew experience).
- Your accepted letter of resignation from your current employer.

Once again, the requirements are different for each airline, and you should not start preparing any documents until you receive the instructions to do so.

2.3.3 DATE OF JOINING (DOJ)

Once all the required documents were submitted and medical tests cleared, you will receive a final acceptance call or email. You will learn about your date of joining - the day you leave towards your new base is officially the day you started working for the airline.

The airline will send an email with a copy of your e-ticket and visa. You will travel from the airport closest to your home. Transport to the airport will not be arranged by the airline.

2.3.4 DOCUMENTS TO PREPARE FOR YOUR DEPARTURE

This list of papers is different from airline to airline, but most will include the following:
- Your highest education diploma in original and copies.
- A copy of your birth certificate.
- Copies of the birth certificates of your siblings (the mother and father name should be mentioned in it).
- Passport copies for all your immediate family (parents, siblings, spouse, children, as applicable).
- The original medical forms, reports, and X-rays.
- Passport photographs (the number and specifications for each airline are different, you will receive the details in your successful candidate email).

All the documents will be placed in your HR file.

CHAPTER 3 – OFF YOU GO!

3.1 FAMILY AND FRIENDS

Telling your family and friends that you will be relocating to another country is one of the most emotional things you have to do. You are about to embark on exploring unknown territory. You will always have some people supporting you and others who will not agree with your choice.

There will be goodbye parties, tears and promises to keep in touch and come back home whenever you can or have friends visiting you as soon as possible.

I met a girl who was successful in her interview, but her boyfriend was against the move. She wanted to save the relationship and declined the job. She regretted every day her decision, and eventually, the relationship ended. She had to restart the entire process of becoming a flight attendant.

You will have friends you will lose contact with. This is a normal part of the process, but it is certainly not the easiest. Being present on a daily basis and being able to participate in each other's life events is important.

You will also find new friends where you go - you will share your new apartment with somebody else, have batch-mates and meet new people on flights every day.

The people who truly love you, will respect your decision and support you all the way. Make a commitment to keep in touch with your loved ones.

3.2 WHAT TO PACK

You will be given a joining cargo allowance. Bellow, you will find a sample list of stuff to pack. Bear in mind that you are not going to a deserted island and there will be shops to buy your daily essentials from. Do not pack shampoo, soap or food. Also, pack only one set of your winter clothes for layovers.

Let's start first with what you will be provided by the airline in your new apartment:
- furniture
- bedsheets, pillows and duvets
- fully equipped kitchen, including utensils, pots, and pans
- TV
- washer and dryer

The list below covers the minimum items. You will need outfits to go through the first weeks of training until you receive your uniform. Think business attire, similar to the outfit you wore for your final interview.

Before you start packing, be reminded that you are going to a Muslim country. You are expected to dress conservatively. Do not take with you revealing clothing such as very short dresses or skirts, see-through items or deep cleavage tops.
- One suit in a dark color
- 3 shirts
- One dark shoe (closed pattern)
- 1 pair of jeans
- One pair of linen pants or other easy fabric
- 5-10 tops
- One casual jacket
- One pair of casual shoes
- One pair of sandals or flip flops
- One elegant outfit (for going out)
- undergarments
- socks
- pantyhose (you will need many pairs of these)
- gym clothes
- swimming suit
- PJs
- 1-2 towels
- hair accessories (hair dryer, brush, comb, clips, and pins)
- skin accessories (shaver, creams, make-up)
- mobile phone (make sure it is not blocked to work only on the network in your home country)
- laptop and whatever other electronics you consider necessary

- chargers
- travel adapter
- dictionary (English-your language. You will need this most during the initial training.)

3.3 NEW PLACE CALLED HOME

When traveling to your new base, you might be given a chance to fly with your new airline. You will observe the crew and be blown away by the fantastic product that is available for the customers. You will soon be delivering the same fantastic service. Tell the cabin crew that you are a new joiner. They will be very happy to welcome you and already give you some tips about the city, accommodation or training.
Once you arrive, you will have to go through the immigration and pick up your luggage. An airline representative will be waiting for you with a welcome package. You will get all the information about what will happen in the next days, when your training will start and when you will get the first meeting with the rest of your colleagues. You will also receive a sim card with a number that you can start using right away.
You will go to your accommodation. This may be a hotel, a temporary or permanent apartment.
There will be a lot to take in, but if you still have the energy, take a tour and explore your new neighborhood.
The next few days will be hectic. You will go through the medical examination, taking photos, uniform fitting, paperwork, meeting your colleagues and trying to figure out what is happening. Like any other life changing event, this will either make you feel stronger than ever or completely miserable. Whatever the first reaction, be kind to yourself. Everything is new, and it takes a while to adjust.

3.4 THE TRAINING

Once you cleared the medical examination which takes place on the first day at the training academy, you will start the AB-Initio Training (Airline Basics Initiation Training)
This training is designed for the fleet you are assigned to. It will consist of familiarization with the safety and security procedures of the airline, first aid and service training.

You will be participating in this training together with 10-12 other new cabin crew. Together you will have a batch number, and refer to each other as batch-mates.
The training is similar to all middle eastern airlines. The safety training complies with the National Civil Aviation Authority and specially designed for the airline and the different aircraft.
Here are some of the modules that you will go through:

Safety and Emergency Procedures - SEP
This is the most extensive part of the training. In this module, you will learn which safety equipment we have in each aircraft, when and how to use them, survival skills in different environments, emergency procedures onboard the plane - fire, smoke, decompression and evacuation procedures.
There is a very thick manual to go through and new information to assimilate.
At the end of each module, you will have an exam. Most questions are multiple choice, plus a diagram of the all equipment location in the aircraft.
You will also have a practical session on how to open and close the aircraft doors, how to prepare the doors for flight and how to evacuate the plane. You will be scored based on your knowledge and confidence.
This training will take 10-15 days.

Security Training
Airline security is an extremely important part for any airline staff. You will learn how to properly search the aircraft before the passengers embark and also after they disembark.
You will also find out how to deal with potential disruptive passengers and what are people allowed to carry on board the aircraft.
You will need to pass a multiple-choice exam at the end of the session.
This training will take 1-2 days.

Aviation Health
This is your basic medical training. You will learn how to help people who are not feeling well in the aircraft, what basic medication is available in the first aid kits and when to administer it, most common health occurrences and how to recognize them, basic life-saving procedures and health precautions.
At the end of this training, you will also have an exam and a practical session to show your skills on administering CPR and operating a defibrillator.
This training will last 4-5 days.

Crew Resource Management (CRM)
This training will teach you how to properly communicate with all your colleagues in the aircraft, from your fellow crew members, crew seniors, pursers (or cabin managers) and pilots. The purpose of CRM is to create an environment of open, efficient and honest communication regardless of your rank.
This training will last one day.

Service Training
The service training will last 3-4 weeks. It will be intense to learn everything from scratch. At the end of this training, you will be able to deliver the airline's tailored service at the highest standard. It is different for every flight, and there is a different service sequence for a breakfast service, a dinner service or just a bar service. You will also get familiar with basic food and beverage knowledge, cocktail preparation and serving suggestions, standards of food hygiene, duty-free sales, in-flight entertainment system operation; frequent flier program and the airline's tailored customer service and expectations and the company value that you are expected to implement at all times.

Grooming Training
This one-day training will teach you the company's standards of grooming. You will learn how to put your make-up, do your hair, take care of your skin while flying, when should you wear your high-heeled shoes or cabin shoes, when to wear your uniform jacket and when you can remove your hat.

It is a fun day, and you will get a chance to see how many steps the flight attendants go through to look their best.

All the training will be conducted in the airline's state of the art training academy.

After you complete your training, you will need to operate a couple of flights as a supernumerary crew (suppy flights). You will be observing how the job is done in real life, assist in the service and demonstrate that you have the knowledge to operate the equipment in the actual environment of the aircraft. You will be overwhelmed by the speed and complexity of the job, but soon enough you will feel very comfortable in the aircraft.

Once you completed the supernumerary (suppy) flights, your Cabin Crew Flying License will be released by the Civil Aviation Authority, and you will be now a fully qualified Flight Attendant.

Congratulations!!!

SEE YOU UP THERE!

It has been a long journey. There were times when you wanted to give it all up and just put this fantasy in a box to reach only in your imagination. You overcame that, and you have achieved your dream: You are now a flight attendant! Your life will be filled with excitement. You will see places you only saw on TV or in books. You will visit countries and cities you never even knew existed. You will meet amazing people. You will stay in luxurious hotels and learn to move around in new cities like they are your second home.

Enjoy every moment of this fantastic journey!

I had the time of my life flying, and I firmly believe everybody has the right to do what they love. I adored writing this book, and I remember every single new cabin crew I had the privilege to mentor. Thank you for allowing me to help you through this.

Printed in Great Britain
by Amazon